FEMI

Since it began in the 1970s, feminist film theory has revolutionized the way that films and their spectators can be understood. This book focuses on the groundbreaking work of Laura Mulvey, Kaja Silverman, Teresa de Lauretis, and Barbara Creed. Each of these thinkers has opened up a new and distinctive approach to the study of film and this book provides the most detailed account so far of their ideas. It illuminates the following six key concepts and demonstrates their value as tools for film analysis:

- the male gaze
- the female voice
- technologies of gender
- queering desire
- the monstrous-feminine
- masculinity in crisis

Shohini Chaudhuri shows how these four thinkers construct their theories through their reading of films as well as testing their ideas with a number of other examples from contemporary cinema and television. She concludes that the concepts have not remained static over the past thirty years but have continually evolved with the influence of new critical debates and developments in film production, signalling their continuing impact and relevance in an era that is often unthinkingly branded as 'post-feminist'.

Shohini Chaudhuri is Lecturer in Contemporary Writing and Film at the University of Essex. Her articles have appeared in *Screen*, *Camera Obscura*, and *Strategies: Journal of Theory, Culture and Politics*. She has recently published a book called *Contemporary World Cinema: Europe, the Middle East, East Asia and South Asia* (2005).

ROUTLEDGE CRITICAL THINKERS

Series Editor: Robert Eaglestone, Royal Holloway,
University of London

Routledge Critical Thinkers is a series of accessible introductions to key
figures in contemporary critical thought.

With a unique focus on historical and intellectual contexts, the
volumes in this series examine important theorists':

- significance
- motivation
- key ideas and their sources
- impact on other thinkers

Concluding with extensively annotated guides to further reading,
Routledge Critical Thinkers are the student's passport to today's most
exciting critical thought.

Already available:

For further details on this series, see www.routledge.com/literature/series.asp

FEMINIST FILM THEORISTS

LAURA MULVEY
KAJA SILVERMAN
TERESA DE LAURETIS
BARBARA CREED

Shohini Chaudhuri

Routledge
Taylor & Francis Group

LONDON AND NEW YORK

First published 2006
by Routledge
2 Park Square, Milton Park, Abingdon, Oxon OX14 4RN

Simultaneously published in the USA and Canada
by Routledge
711 Third Avenue, New York, NY 10017

*Routledge is an imprint of the Taylor & Francis Group,
an informa business*

© 2006 Shohini Chaudhuri

Typeset in Perpetua by
Florence Production Ltd, Stoodleigh, Devon

British Library Cataloguing in Publication Data
A catalogue record for this book is available from the British
Library

Library of Congress Cataloging in Publication Data
Chaudhuri, Shohini.
  Feminist film theorists: Laura Mulvey, Kaja Silverman,
  Teresa de Lauretis, Barbara Creed / Shohini Chaudhuri.
      p. cm. – (Routledge critical thinkers)
    Includes bibliographical references and index.
  1. Feminism and motion pictures. 2. Feminist film criticism.
  3. Mulvey, Laura. 4. Silverman, Kaja. 5. De Lauretis, Teresa.
  6. Creed, Barbara. ⸳ I. Title. II. Series.
  PN1995.9.W6C495 2006
  791.43'015082–dc22   2006014097

ISBN10: 0–415–32432–7 (hbk)
ISBN10: 0–415–32433–5 (pbk)
ISBN10: 0–203–35702–7 (ebk)

ISBN13: 978–0–415–32432–8 (hbk)
ISBN13: 978–0–415–32433–5 (pbk)
ISBN13: 978–0–203–35702–6 (ebk)

CONTENTS

SERIES EDITOR'S PREFACE

The books in this series offer introductions to major critical thinkers who have influenced literary studies and the humanities. The *Routledge Critical Thinkers* series provides the books you can turn to first when a new name or concept appears in your studies.

Each book will equip you to approach these thinkers' original texts by explaining their key ideas, putting them into context and, perhaps most importantly, showing you why they are considered to be significant. The emphasis is on concise, clearly written guides that do not presuppose a specialist knowledge. Although the focus is on particular figures, the series stresses that no critical thinker ever existed in a vacuum but, instead, emerged from a broader intellectual, cultural and social history. Finally, these books will act as a bridge between you and their original texts: not replacing them but, rather, complementing what they wrote. In some cases, volumes consider small clusters of thinkers working in the same area, developing similar ideas or influencing each other.

These books are necessary for a number of reasons. In his 1997 autobiography, *Not Entitled*, the literary critic Frank Kermode wrote of a time in the 1960s:

> On beautiful summer lawns, young people lay together all night, recovering from their daytime exertions and listening to a troupe of Balinese musicians.

Under their blankets or their sleeping bags, they would chat drowsily about
the gurus of the time ... What they repeated was largely hearsay; hence my
lunchtime suggestion, quite impromptu, for a series of short, very cheap books
offering authoritative but intelligible introductions to such figures.

There is still a need for 'authoritative and intelligible introductions',
but this series reflects a different world from the 1960s. New thinkers
have emerged and the reputations of others have risen and fallen, as
new research has developed. New methodologies and challenging ideas
have spread through the arts and humanities. The study of literature
is no longer – if it ever was – simply the study and evaluation of
poems, novels, and plays. It is also the study of the ideas, issues, and
difficulties that arise in any literary text and in its interpretation. Other
arts and humanities subjects have changed in analogous ways.

With these changes, new problems have emerged. The ideas and
issues behind these radical changes in the humanities are often presented without reference to wider contexts or as theories that you
can simply 'add on' to the texts you read. Certainly, there's nothing
wrong with picking out selected ideas or using what comes to hand –
indeed, some thinkers have argued that this is, in fact, all we can do.
However, it is sometimes forgotten that each new idea comes from
the pattern and development of somebody's thought and it is important to study the range and context of their ideas. Against theories
'floating in space', the *Routledge Critical Thinkers* series places key
thinkers and their ideas firmly back in their contexts.

More than this, these books reflect the need to go back to the
thinkers' own texts and ideas. Every interpretation of an idea, even
the most seemingly innocent one, offers its own 'spin', implicitly or
explicitly. To read only books on a thinker, rather than texts by that
thinker, is to deny yourself a chance of making up your own mind.
Sometimes what makes a significant figure's work hard to approach is
not so much its style or content as the feeling of not knowing where
to start. The purpose of these books is to give you a 'way in' by
offering an accessible overview of these thinkers' ideas and works and
by guiding your further reading, starting with each thinker's own texts.
To use a metaphor from the philosopher Ludwig Wittgenstein
(1889–1951), these books are ladders, to be thrown away after you
have climbed to the next level. Not only, then, do they equip you to
approach new ideas, but also they empower you, by leading you back

to a theorist's own texts and encouraging you to develop your own informed opinions.

Finally, these books are necessary because, just as intellectual needs have changed, the education systems around the world – the contexts in which introductory books are usually read – have changed radically, too. What was suitable for the minority higher education system of the 1960s is not suitable for the larger, wider, more diverse, high technology education systems of the twenty-first century. These changes call not just for new, up-to-date introductions but new methods of presentation. The presentational aspects of *Routledge Critical Thinkers* have been developed with today's students in mind.

Each book in the series has a similar structure. They begin with a section offering an overview of the life and ideas of the featured thinkers and explaining why they are important. The central section of the books discusses the thinkers' key ideas, their context, evolution and reception: with the books that deal with more than one thinker, they also explain and explore the influence of each on each. The volumes conclude with a survey of the impact of the thinker or thinkers, outlining how their ideas have been taken up and developed by others. In addition, there is a detailed final section suggesting and describing books for further reading. This is not a 'tacked-on' section but an integral part of each volume. In the first part of this section you will find brief descriptions of the key works by the featured thinkers; then, following this, information on the most useful critical works and, in some cases, on relevant websites. This section will guide you in your reading, enabling you to follow your interests and develop your own projects. Throughout each book, references are given in what is known as the Harvard system (the author and the date of a work cited are given in the text and you can look up the full details in the bibliography at the back). This offers a lot of information in very little space. The books also explain technical terms and use boxes to describe events or ideas in more detail, away from the main emphasis of the discussion. Boxes are also used at times to highlight definitions of terms frequently used or coined by a thinker. In this way, the boxes serve as a kind of glossary, easily identified when flicking through the book.

The thinkers in the series are 'critical' for three reasons. First, they are examined in the light of subjects that involve criticism: principally, literary studies or English and cultural studies, but also other disciplines that rely on the criticism of books, ideas, theories and unquestioned assumptions. Second, they are critical because studying their work will provide you with a 'tool kit' for your own informed critical reading and thought, which will make you critical. Third, these thinkers are critical because they are crucially important: they deal with ideas and questions that can overturn conventional understandings of the world, of texts, of everything we take for granted, leaving us with a deeper understanding of what we already knew and with new ideas.

No introduction can tell you everything. However, by offering a way into critical thinking, this series hopes to begin to engage you in an activity which is productive, constructive, and potentially life-changing.

ACKNOWLEDGEMENTS

Many thanks to Margherita Sprio, Oliver Craske, Howard Finn, Martine Dempsey, Jeremy Evans, and William Teatheridge, who offered help and support while I was writing this book.

WHY MULVEY, SILVERMAN, DE LAURETIS, AND CREED?

Since its inception in the 1970s, feminist film theory has provided the impetus for some of the most exciting developments in Film Studies. Feminist film theory almost became the orthodoxy of film theory, such was its influence in the field. Its impact began to be felt in filmmaking itself, with a number of avant-garde and independent and some mainstream films linking theory to practice. Today, however, many believe that the work of feminism is over. Amidst a generalized cultural backlash against feminism since the 1980s, there has, within Film Studies, been a reaction against feminist film theory also – as indeed against all film theory – due to its complex language and abstract concepts. This book is written out of the conviction that despite its considerable complexity there is much to be gained from reconsidering feminist film theory at the present moment, for it can still enrich our experience of films, giving us valuable tools for analysis. When it arrived in the 1970s, it marked a significant leap in the way films and their spectators can be understood. Since then, its theories have not remained static but have absorbed new critical debates as well as responding to developments in film production. This book focuses on the groundbreaking ideas of four major theorists: Laura Mulvey (b. 1941), Kaja Silverman (b. 1947), Teresa de Lauretis (b. 1938), and Barbara Creed (b. 1943), whose work is informed by a passionate commitment to both film and feminism. It will help readers understand the significance of these theorists, who have all made distinctive contributions to feminist film theory, showing why film is a feminist issue and why feminist issues are still important in film.

Although more than thirty years have elapsed since Laura Mulvey's pioneering essay 'Visual Pleasure and Narrative Cinema' (1975), many of its insights still apply to film production today. The representation of 'Woman' as a spectacle to be looked at pervades visual culture. In such representations, 'Woman' is defined solely in terms of sexuality, as an object of desire, in relation to, or as a foil for, 'Man'. Mulvey's 1975 essay explored the inscription of this tendency in mainstream narrative cinema, where it arguably has the most far-reaching effects. She argued that mainstream cinema is constructed for a male gaze, catering to male fantasies and pleasures. Uncovering the voyeuristic and fetishistic responses of male spectators to images of women, the essay was the first attempt to consider the interplay between the spectator and the screen in feminist terms.

Written in a deliberately polemical spirit and suffused with the energies of the Women's Liberation Movement in Britain, Mulvey's essay placed a feminist agenda at the heart of film-theoretical debates, goading critics to reply to her again and again. It has generated such a huge response that it must surely rank amongst the most provocative academic essays ever written. At that time, the pioneers of feminist film theory in Britain were swiftly overtaking their counterparts in the US and imbibing the stimulus of psychoanalytic and semiotic theory from the Continent. 'Visual Pleasure and Narrative Cinema' was published in the British journal *Screen*, which became an important forum of intellectual exchange between British and French film theory. The success of this essay has sometimes led to the mistaken impression that it is Mulvey's only significant work. However, she has written other important essays, including those collected in *Visual and Other Pleasures* (1989) and *Fetishism and Curiosity* (1996), where she critiques her earlier arguments in the light of critical response.

Silverman, de Lauretis, and Creed have all made significant contributions to the debates that Mulvey initiated. Others, notably Mary Ann Doane, Annette Kuhn, bell hooks, and Linda Williams, have had a major influence too. However, Silverman, de Lauretis, and Creed not only exemplify some of the major strands in feminist film theory of the 1980s and 1990s, they have also opened up distinctive approaches within the field which have impacted even beyond Western film theory.

The work of Kaja Silverman, an American theorist, shares the Continental influences of the British theorists and in particular develops the thinking of the French psychoanalyst Jacques Lacan (1901–81) for feminist purposes. Her book *The Acoustic Mirror* (1988) departs from ongoing feminist debates about the 'gaze' and whether it is male by extending the feminist critique of narrative cinema into the area of the voice, including the question of authorial voice. In another of her influential texts, *Male Subjectivity at the Margins* (1992), she deals with the phenomenon of male masochism and other forms of male subjectivity that exhibit classically 'feminine' traits. In the process, she exposes the ideological vulnerability of so-called masculine 'norms', showing masculinity itself to be a representational category, not unlike femininity.

Teresa de Lauretis was born and educated in Italy before emigrating to the US. Her work stands out for its considered critique of the psychoanalytic paradigms that dominate feminist film-theoretical debates. Although not anti-psychoanalytic, she draws on an alternative theoretical base for her concept of the technology of gender, which seeks to go further than either the work of cultural historian Michel Foucault (1926–84) from which it is derived or existing psychoanalytically-informed feminist theories which appeared unable to address the different experiences of women with regard to race, sexuality, and class. De Lauretis's work on lesbian desire moreover exemplifies the dialogue between feminist and queer theory, which – in the aftermath of Mulvey's controversial essay – developed its own debates on gender and sexuality, the gaze and visual pleasure, partly as a contestation of established feminist views.

Meanwhile, Australian theorist Barbara Creed, whose links are to the Australian Women's Movement, works within a psychoanalytic framework derived from both Sigmund Freud (1856–1939) and the semiotic theorist Julia Kristeva (b. 1941). Creed has extended feminist insights to many aspects of postmodern culture. In particular, she has produced an extremely influential analysis of patriarchal ideology in the horror genre, which abounds with visions of woman as the 'monstrous-feminine'.

INFLUENCES

As a movement, feminism has a diversity of branches and approaches but generally speaking it strives to analyze and change the power structures of patriarchal societies – that is, societies where men rule and where their values are privileged. Feminists make women's position their primary concern, but their analysis of power relations is often relevant to, and encompasses, other subordinated, oppressed, and exploited groups. This means, contrary to most perceptions, that feminism is not just about women nor is it simply 'against' men. Although examples of 'feminist' thought can be found much earlier (notably, Mary Wollstonecraft's *Vindication of the Rights of Woman* [1792]), the suffragette movement of the late nineteenth and early twentieth century is known as feminism's 'First Wave'. Feminist film theory is a product of 'Second Wave' feminism, which began in the 1960s. With the slogan 'the personal *is* the political', the Second Wave drew attention to domains of women's experience hitherto considered non-political and revealed the hidden power structures at work there, including in the home and family, reproduction, language use, fashion, and appearance. Its aim was to transform the entirety of women's condition and not just one aspect, unlike the earlier suffragette movement that exclusively focused on the campaign for women's vote and left other areas of life unchanged.

Although the book predates the movement itself, the starting point for all Second Wave feminist thought is *The Second Sex* (1949), written by the French novelist and philosopher Simone de Beauvoir (1908–86). When de Beauvoir wrote *The Second Sex* she did not identify herself as a feminist, but as a socialist, believing that socialism would bring an end to women's oppression. For her, that belief only changed in 1972 when she joined the *Mouvement de la Libération des Femmes* (MLF), a Marxist-Feminist group in France; it was then that she called herself a feminist for the first time. In 1963 an American journalist, Betty Friedan, published *The Feminine Mystique*, which applied de Beauvoir's insights to postwar (white) Anglo-American women's consciousness and thereby gave Second Wave feminism its initial voice. Friedan's book was hugely influential on the first cluster of feminist film criticism published in the US. The influence of de Beauvoir and Friedan on feminist film theory and criticism will be discussed further in Chapter 1.

In America, Second Wave feminism has roots in the black Civil Rights Movement led by Martin Luther King, the anti-Vietnam War Movement, the student movement and the political Left, which radicalized an entire generation at a time when the American state was becoming violently repressive of internal opposition to its foreign and domestic policies. These movements participated in the tide of radicalism that swept across advanced capitalist countries in the 1960s. Created in the aftermath of the Stonewall riots in 1969 and similarly inspired by the decade's radicalism, the Gay Liberation Movement was also later to impact on feminist thought. Many women who became feminist activists were initially involved in other ideological campaigns. They were reluctant to make women's oppression a separate cause until circumstances compelled them.

Both the civil rights and the anti-war movements were male-dominated. In the 1960s, women in these movements came to realize that they were 'playing the same roles *in* the movement as out of it' – for example, 'making coffee but not policy' (Morgan 1970: xx). Chairman of the Student Nonviolent Coordinating Committee, Stokely Carmichael famously declared in 1966 that 'the only position for a woman in the SNCC is prone' (Morgan 1970: 35). Male campaigners clearly did not include women in their egalitarian ideals. Towards the end of the 1960s, American women activists began to form their own alternative or additional liberation movements. In the 1970s, lesbian feminists in the US and elsewhere were also forced to form their own cause, as they faced sexism from within the ranks of gay liberation as well as homophobia from heterosexual feminists.

Outside America, 1960s radicalism took the form of attacks on universities, workers' strikes and factory occupations, and the Socialist 'New Left' Movement (defined in opposition to the 'old left' of Stalinism and social democracy). One of the key events took place in Paris, May 1968, when student demonstrations and clashes with the police led to workers' strikes across France. In Britain, the Women's Liberation Movement grew out of the British New Left, where women found themselves in a similar position to their US counterparts, thwarted by their fellow male campaigners' unwillingness to extend their ideals to counter women's oppression. The British New Left's strong Marxist influences set it apart from other New Left movements and gave British feminism its special hallmark of socialist commitment, which is evident in British feminist film theory. Juliet Mitchell (b. 1940), one of the British New Left activists who formulated a feminist challenge to traditional Marxism, was a key influence, as we will see in Chapter 1.

Second Wave feminism was extremely effective in obtaining new reproductive and legal rights for women, including, in the UK, the

1975 Sex Discrimination Act, which outlawed discrimination on the grounds of sex in employment, education, and other spheres. However, even today its goal of equal opportunities for men and women remains unachieved in many areas of public life. Although women have entered new trades and professions as a result of the Second Wave's efforts, there is still a gender pay gap disadvantaging women in most professions: for example, in the UK, five years after leaving university women are likely to earn 15 per cent less than men. Many professional women also encounter 'glass ceilings' preventing their promotion beyond a certain stage.

Martha Lauzen's research into the 'celluloid ceiling' has recently brought attention to these problems within the Hollywood film industry. Her statistics reveal that not only are women significantly under-represented behind-the-scenes as directors, cinematographers, editors, producers, and writers but their chances of advancing through the industry are also far less than men's (Lauzen 2005). Since 1990, the Guerrilla Girls feminist group (who formed in 1985) together with some anonymous female directors who call themselves the Alice Locas, have been staging protests revealing that the US senate is more progressive than the Hollywood film industry, where for example only 4 per cent of 2002's top-grossing films were directed by women, compared to 14 per cent female senators (Guerrilla Girls 2003). Whether from Hollywood or elsewhere, few female directors have become household names, unlike a multitude of male directors. Contrary to the claims that feminism's aims have largely been achieved, these examples show that there is a long way to go before powerful women in the arts no longer seem rare. Increased numbers of women directors by themselves would not necessarily transform the dominant means of representation in films, but one is unlikely to occur without the other.

Some feminists reject the goal of equality because it suggests an attempt to aspire to the same condition as men within the existing system. Their aim instead is to bring about a more profound change in values where these kinds of power hierarchies would no longer exist. They espouse a politics of difference, arguing that although women are the same as ('equal to') men in terms of their intellectual capabilities, it is politically *necessary* to assert difference in order to combat a patriarchal culture that devalues and disparages women '*as* women' or tries to collapse them into a male symbolic logic (Moi 1991: 13). Difference is important to the feminist movement because it has become clear that equality politics and legislation alone do not liberate women from patriarchal oppressions.

True to the slogan 'the personal is the political', many of the Second Wave campaigns centred on women's bodies and issues of feminine appearance. As well as putting women's right to control reproduction and motherhood on the agenda, they exposed the exploitation of women in advertisements and beauty contests. This aspect of feminism, together with the popular caricature of women angrily burning their bras (in any case a myth), is often ridiculed today, in the belief that these issues are trivial, including by women who enjoy taking care of their appearance and claim they do it for themselves out of their own free choice. Women's magazines and beauty adverts, too, speak the language of self-emancipation and self-control ('be who you really want to be', 'because you're worth it') yet the 'norms of feminine appearance' they promote are unobtainable for most women (Saul 2003: 144). Cultivated through a continual dependence on expensive beauty products, these impossible ideals are no longer aimed only at affluent Western women: in today's global consumerist market, women in numerous parts of the world are being conditioned to fulfil the same Western feminine ideals. The beauty industry's increased targeting of men, too, does not diminish the problem but rather indicates that the trend has worsened since Second Wave feminists first highlighted it in the 1960s and 1970s.

Inevitably, the legal and medical issue of the woman's body in the Second Wave's political campaigns spilled over into the realm of representation. As Mulvey says, 'women's struggle to gain rights over their bodies could not be divorced from questions of [the] image' (Mulvey 1989a: vii). Along with Kate Millett's *Sexual Politics* (1969) and Shulamith Firestone's *The Dialectic of Sex* (1970), Robin Morgan's anthology *Sisterhood is Powerful* (1970) is one of the key feminist works published at the time. It contains a list of films 'recommended either for their insights into women's problems or into the society that creates problems' – an early indication that film could be an important forum for feminist debate. Listed films include Jean-Luc Godard's *Masculin-féminin* (1966), Michelangelo Antonioni's *Red Desert* (1964), and some Hollywood films starring Rosalind Russell, Katherine Hepburn, and Doris Day (Morgan 1970: 582). In Britain, Laura Mulvey and Claire Johnston (1940–87) joined the London Women's Film Group, which started in 1971 and was devoted to screening films by women. They also helped to organize the first women's film festival in Edinburgh in August 1972, two months after the first International Women's Film Festival held in New York. The festivals coincided with the launch of the first feminist film journal, *Women and Film*, founded by a California-based collective. In quick succession came the first books: Marjorie Rosen's *Popcorn Venus* (1973), Joan Mellen's *Women and their Sexuality in the New Film* (1974), and Molly Haskell's *From Reverence to Rape* (1974). All from the US, Rosen, Mellen and Haskell belong to a strand of feminist criticism that has become known as 'Images of Women', which takes a sociological approach to texts: relating the female characters to historical reality, describing how they form stereotypes and whether or not they offer positive role models for their female audiences.

British feminist film theorists, including Johnston, published their first work, *Notes on Women's Cinema*, in 1973. They rejected the US critics' sociological approach to cinema which, they believed, considered only surface elements of story and character and failed to engage with the specificities of the film medium – for example, how lighting, editing, and camera movement work together with or separately from the stories and characters to create hidden structures or subtexts of meaning. They also did not think that it was so easy to crack the ideological façade and reveal the 'real' women beneath. As we will see in Chapters 1 and 2, Mulvey, along with other British theorists like Johnston, Kuhn and Pam Cook, swerved away from the US trend by using psychoanalysis, French structuralism, and semiotics. In addition to Freud, they drew on thinkers such as Lacan, the Marxist philosopher Louis Althusser (1918–90), the anthropologist Claude Lévi-Strauss (b. 1908), the film theorist Christian Metz (b. 1941), and the semioticians Julia Kristeva and Roland Barthes (1915–80). They used these theoretical discourses to understand *how* films produced their meanings and how they addressed their spectators. They put forward a view of Hollywood cinema as a popular mythology, an unconsciously-held collective patriarchal fantasy, which does not reflect any woman's 'reality' but in which her image functions as a sign.

Meanwhile, in America, a breakaway group from the founding US feminist journal, *Women and Film*, started a new journal, *Camera Obscura*, in 1976. Links established between the Paris Cinématèque and North American universities enabled the *Camera Obscura* collective to attend lectures by Lacan, Barthes, and the film theorists Raymond Bellour and Jean-Louis Baudry (Kaplan 2000: 6). Although the British feminists led the way in turning to French theory, American feminist film theorists now began to take in many of the same influences. The American feminist film theorists' articles also started to appear in other US journals, such as *Jump Cut*, which had been publishing feminist film criticism since it began in 1974. In Britain, the film journal *m/f* appeared in 1978 as a new forum for the feminist film theorists' research. While French thinkers were the dominant stimulus, the British theorists' interpretation of culture as ideology also shows influences of the work of Frankfurt School Marxist philosophers such as Theodor Adorno (1903–69). *Gays and Film* (1977), a pioneering volume of essays published by the British Film Institute and edited by Richard Dyer, became another touchstone of the era. Gay male film critics like Dyer and Robin Wood have increasingly integrated feminist theoretical perspectives into their work. *Gays and Film* later became a founding text for queer theory, which emerged in the 1990s and reasserted allegiances between lesbian and gay critics and theorists. The US-based thinker Teresa de Lauretis, who coined the term queer theory, helped to forge the critical debates on lesbian spectatorship and representation in film in the 1980s and 1990s, along with other theorists such as Judith Mayne (see Chapter 5).

In France, a journal had been founded in the 1950s called *Cahiers du Cinéma*, which did not publish feminist analyses but shaped feminist film theory developing elsewhere. It was closely associated with the French *nouvelle vague* film movement, and many *nouvelle vague* directors, including Jean-Luc Godard and François Truffaut, initially worked as critics on this journal. The critical theory for which the *Cahiers du Cinéma* group are best known is the *politique des auteurs*, translated in Britain and America in the 1960s as '*auteur* theory', a phrase coined by the US film critic Andrew Sarris. This theory basically extends ideas of authorship from literature to the cinema, despite the differences between the two forms, so that a film comes to be seen as the expression of its director's unique style. Ironically, post-structuralist critical theory would soon come to contest the very idea of the author as the source or centre of the text, a position staked out in Roland Barthes's 'The Death of the Author' (1968). Within *Cahiers du Cinéma* itself *auteur* theory did not remain static, but shifted emphasis, especially after the student demonstrations of May 1968, eventually also becoming subject to the influences of semiotics, structuralism, and Marxist ideological criticism. It revolutionized film criticism by placing a new accent on film style and form, rather than mere content, and it critically validated Hollywood cinema as never before, attesting that it was as worthy of attention as art cinema.

Although Hollywood was not the only kind of cinema it championed, it was the one that caught the most attention. For the *Cahiers* group and later for feminist film theorists, the classical Hollywood studio era of the 1930s and 1940s exemplified commercial cinema. The *Cahiers* group listed the Hollywood directors Alfred Hitchcock, Howard Hawks, John Ford, Douglas Sirk, and Nicholas Ray among their prime *auteurs*. To show how Hollywood directors left their stylistic imprint on films made in such a bureaucratic environment where nearly all aspects of production (including subject matter, script, and editing style) were controlled by the studios, the *Cahiers du Cinéma* critics asserted that directors would at least make their own decisions about the *mise en scène*, which is where their personalities would be inscribed. *Mise en scène* is a concept that usually designates everything placed before the camera (lighting, set design, acting, etc.) but the *Cahiers* critics use it more generally to include all aspects of style, including camera placement and camera movement.

Feminist film theorists shared the *Cahiers* critics' love of classical Hollywood cinema, its directors and its genres. Yet they quickly discerned the male bias of this *auteur* theory, which promulgated film criticism in the 'great man' or 'male genius' tradition with no reference to women's images or women's positions in films – a tendency they were keen to remedy. They also set about bringing to light works by women directors in the past. These two goals became the starting point for thinking about a feminist filmmaking practice. Many feminist theorists looked to avant-garde and independent film practice, for example the work of Chantal Akerman and Yvonne Rainer, for possibilities of 're-inventing' cinema, while others hoped for change within mainstream cinema. During the 1980s, feminist film theory became increasingly incorporated into academia and, according to its detractors, more removed from practice. But from this period onwards, it actually became more concerned with women's agency and desires, accommodating many new areas of thought and experience in the process. As the first major developments in feminist film theory happened in Britain and America, I have concentrated on those here. However, those ideas also travelled, by means of books, journals, film festivals, academic courses, and visiting filmmakers and theoreticians, to mainland Europe and Australia, impacting on the work of feminist film theorists there (Creed 1987: 281).

THIS BOOK

Although several critical overviews of feminist film theory exist, these tend to be general accounts. The organization of this volume – focusing on *these* four major figures and *their* ideas – is quite different. *Feminist Film Theorists* illuminates six key concepts that have been influential in feminist film theory over the last three decades – the male gaze, the female voice, technologies of gender, queering desire, the monstrous-feminine, and masculinity in crisis. It will show how the theorists construct their theories through their reading of films as well as testing the theories with a number of other examples.

The Key Ideas section of this book will start by outlining important ideas in the Second Wave feminist movement and the theoretical developments that were absorbed into the beginnings of feminist film theory. Chapter 2 will show how Mulvey's work emerged from the Women's Liberation Movement, laying the foundations for future feminist film debates with her concept of the 'male gaze'. It will examine the way she used psychoanalysis and semiotics to move beyond the 'Images of Women' kind of criticism, to offer a much more provocative and challenging form of feminist film analysis. The following chapters set out the other concepts – the female voice, technologies of gender, queering desire, the monstrous-feminine, and masculinity in crisis – roughly placing them in order of their development. As we shall see, however, Kaja Silverman was investigating masculinity in crisis – a concept that became very popular during the 1990s – as early as 1980. Each chapter focuses on the thinker to whom the concept most belongs and the texts relevant to that concept: Silverman's *Acoustic Mirror* (1988) for Chapter 3, 'The female voice'; de Lauretis's *Alice Doesn't* (1984) and *Technologies of Gender* (1987) for Chapter 4, 'Technologies of gender'; de Lauretis's later book *The Practice of Love* (1994) for Chapter 5, on 'Queering desire'; Creed's writings for Chapter 6, 'The monstrous-feminine'; and Silverman's work on male subjectivity for 'Masculinity in crisis'. Following the Key Ideas section, a final section, 'After Mulvey, Silverman, De Lauretis, and Creed', looks at the continuing impact of these thinkers' work on contemporary theory.

This book seeks to demonstrate the relevance of feminist film theories to a broad variety of cinema and media. Interspersed throughout the chapters are case studies of films from the theorists' own examples as well as other narrative films that are well known or easy to obtain. The book does not seek to replace the theorists' work but to introduce their ideas and lead readers to their texts. For this reason, it ends with a 'Further Reading' section, which lists books by these theorists and provides some information on each, as well as on titles of works by other important feminist film theorists. A few helpful secondary texts are also mentioned, to indicate their usefulness in accompanying study of the primary works.

KEY IDEAS

1

BEGINNINGS

The claim that feminism has now achieved its aims and there is no more work left for it to do has historical echoes. Look at what Simone de Beauvoir wrote in the preface to *The Second Sex*, published in 1949: 'Enough ink has been spilled in the quarrelling over feminism, now practically over, and perhaps we should say no more about it' (de Beauvoir 1993: xxxvi). Ironically, *The Second Sex* is the book that heralded Second Wave feminism – the era in which, as many people would acknowledge, the feminist movement made enormous advances; de Beauvoir made such a statement then because she herself was writing in the midst of an earlier anti-feminist backlash, which grew in the aftermath of the Second World War. *The Second Sex* helped feminism to counter that backlash by giving the Second Wave its intellectual ballast. This chapter elaborates its impact and other diverse ideas that influenced feminist film theory at its beginnings: the theoretical trends that it marshalled for its ends and the problems posed by psychoanalysis. It will look at how feminist film theory and criticism developed the insights of Second Wave feminism, in particular how British feminist film theorists radically reformulated the 'Images of Women' criticism prevalent in the US in the early 1970s. By using theoretical discourses, feminist film theory was able to demonstrate its intellectual rigour, which helped it to establish its position within academia but also allowed it to significantly advance the feminist analysis of film.

THE ETERNAL FEMININE

In *The Second Sex*, de Beauvoir famously wrote that 'one is not born, but rather becomes, a woman' (de Beauvoir 1993: 281). This offered Second Wave feminists the insight that gender is a matter of culture, acquired through social conditioning, rather than being 'natural' or innate. It led them to distinguish, for example, between the word 'female', which specifies biological sex, and the word 'feminine', which describes a *social* gender role. De Beauvoir herself was determined to shatter the myth of 'the eternal feminine' that, she claimed, human civilization has produced. An essence that women are meant to embody, the 'eternal feminine' sometimes refers to a biological essence, at others to a spiritual one. It attributes qualities such as inferiority, gentleness, and emotionality to women, and assumes them to be innate and fixed. For de Beauvoir, on the other hand, no essential characteristic should determine how one becomes a woman.

De Beauvoir's ideas stem from Existentialist philosophy, a school of thought that she helped to form together with Jean-Paul Sartre (1905–80). Sartre argued that human beings exist both *in* themselves and *for* themselves, unlike objects that are simply there, existing only in themselves. In *The Second Sex*, de Beauvoir asserts that men have claimed this subject position for themselves and, in order to ratify themselves in it, they have reduced women to the position of an objectified 'Other', denying women existence for themselves. 'Woman', she wrote, appears to man solely as 'a sexual being', not as an autonomous entity: 'She is defined and differentiated with reference to man and not he with reference to her; she is the incidental, the inessential as opposed to the essential. He is the Subject, he is the Absolute – she is the Other' (de Beauvoir 1993: xxxix–xl).

According to de Beauvoir, man purports to be the universal. He is equated with rationality and transcendence of body. Woman appears as his Other: irrational, tied to the body, in all respects defined in relation to man. For de Beauvoir, the source of this gender hierarchy and sexual inequality is patriarchal culture, as purveyed by 'religion, traditions, language, tales, songs, movies', all of which help compose the way in which people understand and experience the world (de Beauvoir 1993: 275). These are the vehicles for myths, created by men and constructed from their viewpoint, which are then mistaken for 'absolute truth'. Through the ages, male thinkers have sought to explain rather than question the notion of women's inferiority, by recourse to theology, religion, biology, and other 'scientific' dis-courses. They have used the patriarchal myth of the 'eternal feminine' to justify women's oppression.

In 1963 Betty Friedan rebranded the 'eternal feminine' as 'the feminine mystique' and translated de Beauvoir's ideas to an American cultural environment. Her book *The Feminine Mystique* struck an enormous chord with a generation of middle-class women who had been forced back into the roles of mothers and housewives after the Second World War, when they had joined the war effort, performing civilian jobs while men were away. Now, during the postwar consumer boom, these women were being expected to find 'feminine fulfilment' in suburban housekeeping, sexual passivity, male domination, and devotion to their children. For those women, Friedan articulated 'the problem that had no name' – that being confined to the role of housewife was deeply unsatisfying for most women, who longed for something more (Friedan 2001: 15). In her view, education and professional work were the answer.

Friedan's book reiterated how women were defined only in sexual relation to men – this time as 'wife, sex object, mother, housewife' – and never as people defining themselves by their own actions (Friedan 2001: xv). Drawing her examples from popular culture, she argued that this image of 'feminine mystique' bombards us at all times, through magazines, television commercials, mass media, and psychology textbooks. The feminine mystique has socially conditioned women to consent to their roles as mothers and housewives, becoming the 'cherished and self-perpetuating core of American culture', and making women feel guilty for taking a job outside the home – guilty for 'undermining' their husbands' masculinity and their own femininity, and for neglecting the children (Friedan 2001: 18). In this way, the feminine mystique restates the traditional division between virgin and whore in patriarchal representation as the contemporary opposition: housewife versus career woman.

Although Friedan implied connections between the power of images and women's real existence, she left the analysis to be developed by others, including US feminist film critics who conducted the form of reading that has subsequently become known as 'Images of Women' criticism. Before we go on to look at this work and how it was reformulated by British film theorists, there is still one other important feminist influence to discuss: the writings of Juliet Mitchell, a British New Left Member and a pioneer of the British Women's Movement, who put Freud and psychoanalysis on the feminists' political agenda.

PSYCHOANALYSIS AND FEMINISM

In the 1960s, many feminists thought that psychoanalysis was their number one public enemy. Friedan, for example, believed that the feminine mystique 'derived its power from Freudian thought' (Friedan 2001: 103), while others held Freud singularly responsible for the counter-revolution against feminism (Millett 1977: 178). Mitchell argued that the feminist attack on Freud was largely based on misconceptions about his theories perpetuated by pseudo-Freudian ideas in the cultural mainstream – a trend particularly visible in the US where popular versions of psychoanalysis were eagerly embraced and where anti-Freudianism among feminists ran high. These popularizations of psychoanalysis testify to Freud's widespread impact while at the same time censoring his best insights. In her book *Psychoanalysis and Feminism* (1974), Mitchell re-read Freud through the work of the French psychoanalyst Lacan, whom she also introduced to English-speaking readers. She later edited with Jacqueline Rose in 1982 a collection of Lacan's writings on feminine sexuality. Through her, both Lacan and Freud became established as key figures in feminism's dialogue with psychoanalysis. (See Chapter 2 for an initial account of Lacan's ideas.) One reason, Mitchell points out, why Freud is still relevant to us today and why he is not 'the culture-bound product of a small-minded "Victorian" patriarch', as some feminists would have him, is his notion of the unconscious (Mitchell 1990: xx). For Freud, the unconscious is eternal – it will always exist – but that does not mean that it transcends history. The unconscious plays a crucial role in the way we internalize the laws and beliefs of our society. Although these laws and beliefs are themselves subject to cultural change, they have historically laid the foundations of patriarchy. Therefore, Mitchell argues, psychoanalysis is not 'a recommendation for a patriarchal society but an analysis of one' (Mitchell 1990: xv). This makes psychoanalysis indispensable for feminism.

Mitchell's first important contribution to the feminist debate was her essay 'Women: the Longest Revolution', published in the *New Left Review* in 1966, pirate copies of which were widely disseminated in

THE UNCONSCIOUS

Sigmund Freud, the founder of psychoanalysis, emphasized that the motives behind our actions are mostly unconscious. He divided the mind into different layers: the conscious, which contains our present awareness; the preconscious, which contains material that is largely unconscious, but which can be recalled; and the unconscious, which is made up of ideas and representations that are actively repressed, and which do not reach consciousness except in disguised form, as in dreams or slips of the tongue (hence, the notorious 'Freudian slip'). Freud also named three agencies governing the mind: the id, which is the irrational, unconscious part ruled by instinctual drives; the ego, the largely conscious, rational part of the mind, which tries to control the id; and the superego, a part of the ego that acts as a judge or censor and which comes into being as a result of prohibitions learned from our parents, school, or religious authorities. Whatever the ego and superego forbid us to do or think is repressed and driven into the unconscious.

In *The Interpretation of Dreams* (1900), for example, Freud argues that dreams fulfil repressed wishes, but in order to evade the ego's censorship, these wishes are disguised when they reach the waking mind. The latent dream material is 'translated' through processes of 'condensation' (reducing a number of ideas to one image) and 'displacement' (the affect or emotional charge attached to a given set of ideas is detached from them and transferred to a more harmless set of ideas). When the dreamer awakes and tries to recall the dream, it undergoes 'secondary revision': the dreamer tries to make sense of the dream by turning it into a narrative. This produces the dream's 'manifest' content, a significantly disguised version of its latent content, which can, nonetheless, Freud believed, be revealed through psychoanalysis.

the early years of the Women's Liberation Movement. In the essay, later expanded for her book *Woman's Estate* (1971), she criticizes both traditional Marxism and contemporary socialism for not paying proper heed to women's condition. Classical Marxist literature symbolically equates woman's situation with that of society generally; for example, it views woman as a slave before the existence of slavery. Mitchell argues that these ideas do not recognize woman's condition as being different from other social groups. Women's exploitation and subordination takes the form of 'a *specific* structure', involving a unity of different factors combining in different ways at different historical periods (Mitchell 1966: 16). These factors are production, reproduction, sex, and the socialization of children; genuine liberation for women means transforming all four of them.

Unlike Marx, Freud understood that the nuclear family was a key vehicle for the socialization of human individuals into society's gender norms and expectations. We can see this in his theory of 'the Oedipus Complex', named after the Greek tragedy by Sophocles, *Oedipus Rex*, which narrates the story of how Oedipus unknowingly murdered his father and married his mother. In Freud, the Oedipus Complex stands for the loving and hostile wishes any child harbours for its parents. He makes the Oedipus Complex into a key moment in the psychosocial structuring of sexuality and gender, occurring when a child is between the ages of three and five. In the 'positive' version of the Complex, the child desires the parent of the opposite sex and identifies with the parent of the same sex, whom it sees as a rival. Initially, however, children of *both* sexes form an incestuous attachment to the mother, which ends when they discover that she does not possess a penis, as

CASTRATION

This is a key psychoanalytic concept, which – like many other psychoanalytic ideas – can be regarded as a metaphor or myth that helps us to understand how social structures and beliefs are produced. Castration is the 'myth' that children use to explain the origins of sexual difference between the sexes. In this respect it is similar to other fantasies that children or their carers invent to explain the origins of things, for example, the riddle of where babies come from. Freud states: 'It is self-evident to a male child that a genital like his own is to be attributed to everyone he knows, and he cannot make its absence tally with his picture of these people' (Freud 1991b: 113). Boys hold obstinately to this conviction and will only abandon it with a struggle. Substitutes for the penis, which they think is missing in women, play a determining role in many 'perversions' such as fetishism, as we will see in Chapter 2. Girls do not resort to this kind of denial but, in Freud's view, when they see that boys' genitals are different from their own, they are overcome with envy for the penis and wish to be boys themselves (Freud 1991b: 114).

formerly believed, leading them to think (mistakenly) that she has been castrated. Fearing the same punishment at the hands of the jealous father, the little boy renounces his desire for the mother and accepts his father's authority, knowing that one day he will inherit his father's power and possess a woman of his own.

Freud describes girls' different experience of the Oedipus and castration complexes in a way that, it could be argued, explains their lack of access to the cultural privileges enjoyed by men. Upon discovering that the mother is castrated like herself, the little girl is expected to transfer her affections to the father, transforming the wish for a penis into a wish to bear him (and later, her lovers) a male baby. By successfully negotiating this transition, the girl becomes a woman; that is, she enters the culturally sanctioned role of femininity. However, Freud makes it clear that girls never fully complete this Oedipal trajectory and that this socially-enforced way of 'becoming a woman' is fraught with difficulty and resistance.

Feminists have criticized Freud for his reductive understanding of sexual difference as the absence or presence of the penis. Many object to the centrality he gives to the phallus, which has earned him the title of being 'phallocentric' – a term coined by British psychoanalyst Ernest Jones, who disputed the notion of penis envy. For most of his career, Freud struggled to understand femininity. Feminists perceived the 'problem' of femininity in psychoanalysis as symptomatic of the 'problem' of femininity within patriarchal discourse, where it appears either as an absence or measured in terms of male norms. However, feminist advocators of Freud, like Mitchell, pointed out that Freud was a subtler thinker than his detractors imagined. He himself revised and reformulated his theories constantly, aware of their provisional nature. In their turn, feminists who utilize his ideas revise them for their own purposes, while interrogating psychoanalysis as a discourse.

THE TOOLS OF FILM THEORY

This section will look at how early British feminist film theory deployed the language of Freudian psychoanalysis and combined it with the new waves of theories arriving from France: semiotics, Althusserian Marxism, and the work of the post-1968 *Cahiers du Cinéma* critics. Among the pioneers of British feminist film theory, and one of the first to combine these approaches with psychoanalysis, was Claire Johnston.

Johnston helped to organize the women's film festival in Edinburgh in 1972 and wrote the essay 'Women's Cinema as Counter-Cinema' in the accompanying pamphlet *Notes on Women's Cinema*, published in 1973. As mentioned earlier, the turn to theory was part of a reaction against the sociological 'Images of Women' film criticism that had emerged in the early 1970s in the US. This includes the early articles published in the journal *Women and Film* as well as writings by Molly Haskell, Marjorie Rosen, and Joan Mellen. This work was guided by a strong political commitment: 'We are not trying to add a chapter to academic film criticism, we are trying to change our situation', declare the editors Siew-hwa Beh and Saunie Salyer in the second issue of *Women and Film* (Beh and Salyer 1972b: 3). However, they and other early US feminist film critics have been criticized since for their 'reflectionist' approach to film.

For example, articles in *Women and Film* look upon film 'as a kind of mirror which reflects a changing society', albeit a mirror that 'has always been limited in its reflection, and possibly distorted' (Mohanna 1972: 7). This distortion is said to be invariably of 'a masculine viewpoint'. Focusing on negative female stereotypes such as prostitute, wife, mother, vamp, or *femme fatale*, this kind of criticism is a monolithic attack on the 'system' of Hollywood film. Its movies are thought to generate false consciousness, encouraging women to adopt and identify with the false images they perpetuate and reinforce. The *Women and Film* writers hold the belief that 'when the stereotypes fade' or when there are more women filmmakers, 'the reflection we see on screen will be really transformed' (Mohanna 1972: 7). Women will be portrayed as they are, rather than as 'servile caricatures' (Beh and Salyer 1972a: 6).

In 'Women's Cinema As Counter Cinema', Johnston responds directly to the early issues of *Women and Film* and other 'Images of Women' analyses, highlighting the problems of their approach. First of all, in claiming that cinema holds up a mirror to reality, they assume that cinema is a transparent medium of communication. Johnston rejects the sociological approach, which evaluates filmic images of women in relation to 'real' women, because cinema is an *artificial* construction, which mediates 'reality' with its own signifying practices. Images appear on our screens transformed by processes of disguise and displacement similar to those uncovered by psychoanalysis. In other words, they appear coded, requiring the help of psychoanalysis and other theories to *de*code them. Johnston emphasizes that cinema is not a transparent window onto the world but a method of communication in which meanings are formed in and by the films themselves. This also puts in question the idea, implied by the *Women and Film* critics, that female stereotypes are the conscious strategy of a male-dominated film industry.

Johnston moreover queried the sociological film critics' demand for 'positive' or 'true' images of women. Is this a demand for images of women as they 'really' are or how we would wish them to be? It also assumes that there is an 'essence' of women that has failed to make it onto the screen due to patriarchal ideology and that this would be rectified if women were allowed to represent themselves realistically. As we have seen with de Beauvoir and Friedan, patriarchy itself has long promoted the idea of a feminine essence, which has been used to rationalize women's oppression and prevent them from changing their situation. Johnston also finds problematic the sociological critics' valorization of realism. For realism, too, is a construction, one that uses its codes and conventions to *conceal* its constructedness. A realist film leads its audiences to believe that its meanings are transparent, requiring no work of interpretation, but all the while the audience is involved in constructing its meanings through the codes they have learned to internalize. For example, a classic Hollywood film appears effortless to watch, offering a transparent 'window' onto its fictional world, yet its 'realism' is created through the working of particular codes, such as the 'invisible' style of continuity editing, with its rules of the axis of action (180 degree rule), eye-line match, and 30 degree rule. All of these maintain the illusion of a seamless spatial and temporal flow from shot to shot and hide the constructedness of the film artefact. Art cinema, too, may use codes of realism – albeit different ones from Hollywood realism – such as long takes or direct address to the camera. These, too, are codes that belong to the ideological repertoire of realism and are no more 'natural', strictly speaking, than Hollywood codes.

These very different ideas about how films work arrived in Britain from Europe, via theoretical writings published in *Screen* in the early 1970s. Johnston and other feminist film theorists saw that theories such as semiotics, Althusserian Marxism, and psychoanalysis could be used as tools for their analyses, allowing them to ask not only *what* films mean but also *how* and *why*. They derived the idea that the spectator

AXIS OF ACTION (180 DEGREE RULE), EYE-LINE MATCH, AND 30 DEGREE RULE

These are all aspects of continuity editing, designed to ensure a smooth temporal and spatial flow from shot to shot. The axis of action (or 180 degree rule) is an imaginary line across the action; within a given scene, all camera placements must be on one side of this line in order to maintain consistency of background and screen direction. Eye-line match is the term for a cut where Shot A shows someone looking offscreen while Shot B shows us what they see; it refers to the positions and the trajectory of the characters' eye-lines, guiding the audience's understanding of the spatial relationships from shot to shot. The 30 degree rule pertains to the minimum change of angle required for a new camera placement; if the change is any less than this, the result is a jump cut which can be disorienting for the audience.

takes part in the production of a film's meanings – and that he or she is also, in the process, constructed by the film itself – from the Marxist philosopher Louis Althusser. He argued that ideology is not a matter of true or false consciousness – one cannot simply 'see through' a false distortion of reality in order to perceive things 'as they really are', for our relationship to reality itself is imaginary. Thus, as he defines it, ideology is a '"representation" of the imaginary relationship of individuals to their real conditions of existence' (Althusser 1999: 123). It is this imaginary relationship that underlies the distortion we see in ideology.

Another tool mobilized in feminist film theory is semiotics – the study of signs, also known as 'semiology' (as explained in the box on Structuralism on page 28) – which can show how ideology operates in a film through its textual codes. A semiotic reading of a film analyzes how its meanings are constructed at a deeper level, through the interplay of its codes of lighting, editing, scale of shot, camera angles, dialogue, and narrative. The key theoretical influence here is Roland Barthes's *Mythologies* (1957), which proposes that all aspects of life, from steak and chips to cinema and fashion, could be understood as sign-systems. Barthes shows how these apparently innocent things are steeped in ideological beliefs; for him, myth is a signifier of ideology. In his analysis of myth, he relies on the distinction between denotation

ALTHUSSER AND IDEOLOGY

The notion of ideology is central to Marxist theory. Broadly defined, ideology refers to a set of ideas and beliefs held by individuals or groups. Often these are ideas that legitimate the power of a dominant social group. In *The German Ideology* (1845–46), Karl Marx and Friedrich Engels characterized ideology as a *camera obscura*, which captures an illusion of reality, yet in it real social relations are presented in 'inverted' form, i.e. distorted. Because the *camera obscura* is a prototype of the cinema, this Marxist model is very influential in film theory. It has even been adopted as the title of a prominent feminist film journal, *Camera Obscura*, which replaced *Women and Film*.

The twentieth-century Marxist philosopher Louis Althusser formulated another very influential notion of ideology in his essay, 'Ideology and Ideological State Apparatuses' (1970). Forging powerful links between Marxism and psychoanalysis, particularly the ideas of Jacques Lacan, this essay has had a strong impact on intellectual discourses since the 1960s. In the essay, Althusser also argues that a state maintains its power both through *repressive* state apparatuses (government, army, police, law courts, prisons), which work through physical force, and *ideological* state apparatuses (art, media, schools, family, church, political parties), which promote values that are amenable to the state and consolidate its power. Due to the existence of the ideological state apparatuses, which do their work almost unnoticeably, it appears to us that we freely assent to ideology rather than having it imposed upon us from 'above'. We internalize the values of the status quo without realizing it.

In Althusser's own terminology, ideology 'constitutes' individuals as subjects, i.e. it makes individuals into subjects: he calls this 'interpellation'. Ideology 'recruits' subjects amongst individuals – it is like the proverbial cry of the police calling out to somebody on the street 'Hey, you there!' making the individual turn round: 'By this mere one-hundred-and-eighty-degree physical conversion, he becomes a *subject*. Why? Because he has recognized that the hail was "really" addressed to him, and that "it was *really him* who was hailed"' (Althusser 1999: 30). Interpellation produces subjects who recognize their own existence in the dominant ideology and therefore freely consent to be in it – Althusser took this as evidence that subjects are always already inside ideology, even before they are born.

(obvious or literal meaning, conveying fact) and connotation (implied or associated meanings). These can be related to the Freudian dream-work, which distinguishes between the manifest and latent content of dreams: both texts and signs can be said to have a latent content. Connotative meanings can be seen as the unconscious of a text and, as in Freud's theory of the unconscious, they are culturally and historically determined. Barthes's famous example is a picture of a black soldier saluting the French flag on the cover of the magazine *Paris Match*. The overt, *denotative* meaning of the picture is simply this: *a black soldier is giving the French salute*. But there is a second level of countless *connotative* meanings relating to ideas of 'France', 'empire', 'race', and so on. Barthes argues that a sign can be stripped of its original denotative meaning so that another, connotative meaning can be laid over it and take its place. This allows the new connotation to be mistaken for the obvious and natural denotation. In this way, it signifies ideologically. This is what has happened in the magazine cover: the connotative meaning signifies that France is a great empire, under which all faithfully serve, regardless of their colour (Barthes 1993: 116).

Barthes characterizes myth as a type of speech, one which is 'chosen by history' rather than evolving from the 'nature' of things (Barthes 1993: 110). To our society, a bunch of roses means passion, but roses have no intrinsic connection to passion. Myth has built a second semiological level to this sign, 'rose', which has become welded together with a new concept or signifier, 'passion', to create a new sign. Semiotic analysis can demystify the signs that are imposed on us as natural. It is not difficult to see why feminist film theorists adopted it for their analysis of 'Woman' as a sign. Myth divests the sign 'Woman' of its denotative meaning (a human being or person with the potential for bearing children) and replaces it with connotative meanings, such as 'Woman as Other', 'the eternal feminine', or 'object of male desire', which give the air of being woman's 'natural' characteristics when in fact they have been constructed through patriarchal discourse (Creed 1987: 300). Johnston comments: 'myth transmits and transforms that ideology of sexism and renders it invisible' (Johnston 2000: 24). Woman becomes a sign for what she represents for man: 'despite the enormous emphasis placed on woman as spectacle in the cinema, woman as woman is largely absent' (Johnston 2000: 25).

With this understanding of cinema, Johnston questions the view that Hollywood is more ideologically oppressive than European art cinema, where sexist stereotyping is less obvious. Hollywood cinema uses iconography – visual and stylistic motifs making up a system of signs based on genre conventions – to build its mythical female stereotypes. But Johnston argues that Hollywood's reliance on iconography actually makes it easier to deconstruct its films' mythic qualities. Moreover, it is possible to deploy icons 'in the face of and against the mythology usually associated with them' (Johnston 2000: 23). This is how she views the work of female directors from Hollywood's past, such as Dorothy Arzner, Lois Weber, and Ida Lupino. She shows how, either by detaching icon from myth or by generating internal contradictions that disrupt the fabric of their films, these female Hollywood directors have managed to bring the sexist ideology in the construction of women out into the open, thereby creating a form of women's counter-cinema.

Johnston's notion of counter-cinema is indebted to a *Cahiers du Cinéma* editorial by Jean-Luc Comolli and Jean Narboni, 'Cinema/Ideology/Criticism', published in 1969 and translated shortly afterwards in *Screen*. Comolli and Narboni suggest that a text can offer a critique of itself through the contradictions that appear between its overt ideology and its formal properties of image, narrative, and dialogue. In such texts, 'an internal criticism is taking place which cracks the film apart at the seams' (Comolli and Narboni 1999: 757). This can be observed, they claim, in many Hollywood films, which 'while being completely in the system and the ideology end up partially dismantling the system from within'. This is far removed from the monolithic attack on the Hollywood 'system' witnessed in early issues of *Women and Film*.

In *Women and Film*, the editors also dismissed *auteur* theory as chauvinistic, 'making the director a superstar as if filmmaking were a one-man show' (Beh and Salyer 1972a: 6). Johnston agrees that the idea of film as the creative expression of its 'artist' is a limiting one that she does not intend to apply to women's filmmaking. However, she does affirm later interventions into *auteur* theory, which remove it from romantic ideas of creativity and intentionality, such as Peter Wollen's *Signs and Meanings in the Cinema* (1972). Here, a director's body of work is said to be unified 'through the force of his preoccupations', which reveal 'unconscious, unintended meanings' to be 'decoded in the film, usually to the surprise of the individual' (cited in Johnston 2000: 26). Johnston shows how this more sophisticated model of *auteur* theory allows us to go beyond the kind of analysis that looks for 'positive' or 'negative' images of women. She shows that the image of woman takes on different meanings in the contexts of different directors' work. For example, in Howard Hawks' films such as *His Girl Friday* (1940) or even *The Thing* (1951), heroines seem to be portrayed 'positively' – they are feisty, aggressive, and independent career women. However, within the film's all-male environments, they figure as 'a traumatic presence which must be negated' (Johnston 2000: 27). In John Ford's Westerns, on the other hand, women represent the desire for settlement, waiting at home for the men who wander off to the frontier; they appear to be more conservative, yet the symbol of woman as civilization enables 'progressive elements' to surface in certain Ford films like *Seven Women* (1966).

Finally, from the anthropologist Lévi-Strauss (b. 1908), Johnston and other feminist film theorists borrowed the idea of symbolic exchange. Lévi-Strauss first set out his ideas in *The Elementary Structures of Kinship* (1949), later to become one of structuralism's founding texts, greatly influencing in particular Lacan. Lévi-Strauss identified a system of exchange practised by primitive people, known as 'exogamy', which he claims laid the foundation of human culture. In this system of exchange, a taboo of incest prohibited women from marrying their own clan members. As a result, women became gifts exchanged between clans – a symbolic way of consolidating trust between different communities. In this exchange, women function as objects rather than partners in the exchange, placing them outside the establishment of the socio-cultural order.

STRUCTURALISM

This movement in critical thought started from the work of Swiss linguist Ferdinand de Saussure (1857–1913), who proposed that language is a system or structure of signs in which the relationship between a sign and its referent (the thing to which it refers) is not intrinsic or 'natural' but based on arbitrary social conventions. Saussure believed that it was possible to extend these principles to *all* types of signs. He called this science of signs 'semiology' – also known as semiotics. His ideas were developed by the anthropologist Claude Lévi-Strauss, who studied kinship structures and the structures of myth, and by Roland Barthes, who applied the science of signs to fashion and other aspects of everyday life.

Lévi-Strauss viewed kinship as a signifying system. Women are the equivalent of signs in that system, circulating between men just as words circulate in language. Therefore, according to Lévi-Strauss, kinship is a type of communication where men 'speak' and women 'are spoken'. The idea that, in patriarchy, women are equivalent to signs spoken by men has been extremely influential for feminist theory. In their essay 'The Place of Woman in the Cinema of Raoul Walsh' (1974), Johnston and Cook use it to illuminate how 'Woman' in Walsh's work is 'the locus of dilemma for the patriarchal human order' – 'a locus of contradictions' (Cook and Johnston 1990: 26). The heroine played by Marlene Dietrich in Walsh's film *Manpower* (1941), for example, appears on the surface to be an independent agent, yet as 'a sign oscillating between the images of prostitute and mother-figure, she represents the means by which the men express their relationship with each other' (Cook and Johnston 1990: 20). At the deeper, structural level, therefore, she functions as an object exchanged between men, existing within their discourse: in these terms, 'she is "spoken", she does not speak'.

SUMMARY

We have seen in this chapter how the political insights into women's oppression of writers such as de Beauvoir, Friedan, and Mitchell laid the basis for critical discussion of women's representation in the media. Feminists first investigated film from a sociological perspective, making direct links between images of women and society – a trend that originated in the US. Dissatisfied with this approach, which they felt did not understand film as a signifying practice, British theorists drew on a number of theoretical discourses that arrived in Britain from France. They sought to analyze the deeper codes and structures governing filmic representations of women. A key figure in this initial undertaking was Claire Johnston, whose work demonstrated the usefulness of psychoanalysis, semiotics, *auteur* theory, Althusserian Marxism, and structural anthropology for revealing a range of hidden meanings in films. She provided the groundwork for the feminist analysis of Woman as a 'sign' signifying the myths of patriarchal discourse and she influentially diagnosed that woman *as* woman remains the unspoken absence of patriarchal culture.

2

THE MALE GAZE

In her article 'Visual Pleasure and Narrative Cinema', written in 1973 and published in *Screen* in 1975, Laura Mulvey argued that the controlling gaze in cinema is always male. Spectators are encouraged to identify with the look of the male hero and make the heroine a passive object of erotic spectacle. Mulvey's concept of the 'male gaze' subsequently became *the* main talking point of feminist film debate. This chapter begins with Mulvey's background in the Woman's Movement and charts her intellectual trajectory from politics to aesthetics. It then goes on to detail her arguments about the male gaze and how film is structured according to male fantasies of voyeurism and fetishism. The chapter will focus on 'Visual Pleasure and Narrative Cinema' but it will also draw on Mulvey's other essays from *Visual and Other Pleasures* (1989) and *Fetishism and Curiosity* (1996). Finally, it will consider Mulvey's 'Afterthoughts' on her arguments about visual pleasure in the light of the critical response to her work, which highlighted issues of female spectatorship.

SEXUAL POLITICS

As I was lifted bodily out of the hall, three Miss Worlds came running up to me, a trio of sequinned, perfumed visions, saying 'Are you all right?', 'Let her go.' When the policeman explained we were from WL [Women's Liberation] and demonstrating against them, I managed to say that we weren't against them, we were for them.

(Mulvey and Jimenez 1989: 5)

At the 1970 Miss World Contest at London's Albert Hall, a group of feminists, hiding leaflets, water-pistols, stink-bombs, and bags of flour in their clothes, secreted themselves among the audience. When the signal was given, they hurled their missiles at the stage. Their protest was broadcast live, gaining the highest viewing ratings that year, before the demo was finally stopped. Among the demonstrators was Mulvey, who recounts the event in 'The Spectacle is Vulnerable: Miss World, 1970', an article co-written with Margarita Jimenez for London's Women's Liberation Workshop journal *Shrew*. The demonstration went successfully, they say in the article, because 'the spectacle isn't prepared for anything other than passive spectators' (Mulvey and Jimenez 1989: 5).

As well as addressing some common misconceptions about what 1970s Women's Liberation was all about, this early article offers a good starting point for the concerns that Mulvey developed into feminist film theory. 'The Miss World competition', Mulvey and Jimenez declare, 'is a public celebration of the traditional female road to success', where women are defined solely by their physical attributes. For Mulvey and her cohorts, sabotaging the Miss World contest meant striking a blow against 'this narrow destiny' and crucially, 'a blow against passivity, not only the enforced passivity of the girls on the stage but the passivity we all felt in ourselves' (Mulvey and Jimenez 1989: 3).

Mulvey's passion for film predates her involvement in the Women's Liberation Movement. Yet it was the Women's Liberation Movement that gave the counterweight to her film theory and filmmaking, compelling her to look at film, especially Hollywood film, through critical eyes and, essentially, enabling her to *write*. Pieces in the journal *Shrew* were written and edited collaboratively and published anonymously, 'a political gesture against the ownership and authority implied by signature' and a way of giving women the 'collective strength . . . to build new means of expression' (Mulvey 1989a: viii). In 'The Spectacle is Vulnerable', Jimenez's personal first-person account is merged with Mulvey's third-person commentary. Despite the dual voice, the specific preoccupations that would embroil Mulvey in the never-ending debates that indelibly bear her name are here in embryonic form: namely, the political campaign involving women's struggle to gain control over their own bodies and how they are represented; the notion of woman as passive spectacle; and the passivity of spectators.

Yet there is a wide gap between this piece and Mulvey's better-known work. In some respects it has more in common with the 'Images of Women' criticism we touched on in the last chapter, with its underlying idea that one can break through the alienating spectacle or façade to women's 'reality' hidden behind it, and that the action of a self-enlightened few are enough to destroy it. It cannot explain what keeps the spectacle in place and what puts women in positions of enforced passivity and moreover makes men and women accept this as natural and inevitable. In other words, it can offer a *description* of ideology but it cannot account for how ideology is *produced* and *perpetuated*. Mulvey's subsequent, more theoretical work takes this next step, drawing on Althusserian Marxism, semiotics, and – most of all – psychoanalysis.

While semiotics led to a way of understanding how images work as signs, psychoanalysis, Mulvey believed, was best placed to unlock 'the mechanics of popular mythology and its raw materials' (xiii). Reflecting on her work fifteen years later, she writes:

Psychoanalytic theory provided ... the ability to see through the surface of cultural phenomena as though with intellectual X-ray eyes. The images and received ideas of run of the mill sexism were transformed into a series of clues for deciphering a nether world, seething with displaced drives and misrecognised desire.

(Mulvey 1989a: xiv)

In 'Visual Pleasure and Narrative Cinema', she remarks on the 'beauty' of psychoanalysis in the way it renders the frustration women experience under 'the phallocentric order' (Mulvey 1989c: 15). The essay is heavily inflected by the theories of Jacques Lacan, who famously stated that 'the unconscious is structured like a language'. Mulvey sets out to uncover the ways in which 'the unconscious of patriarchal society has structured film form' (1989c: 14). This political use of psychoanalysis enables her to turn her focus from the mere description of woman as spectacle to the male psyche whose needs the spectacle serves.

LUST OF THE EYES

The 'magic' of Hollywood, argues Mulvey, lies in its 'skilled and satisfying manipulation of visual pleasure' (Mulvey 1989c: 16). Central to this is what Freud, in his 'Three Essays on the Theory of Sexuality', called 'scopophilia' or 'pleasure in looking' (Freud 1991b: 70). In its active aspect, scopophilia involves taking people as objects for sexual stimulation through sight, 'subjecting them to a controlling and curious gaze' (Mulvey 1989c: 16). An extreme example of this is a Peeping Tom, whose sexual satisfaction is wholly dependent on this activity. Although mainstream cinema is obviously designed for public exhibition, Mulvey suggests that it effectively positions its spectators as Peeping Toms: the darkened auditorium gives each spectator the illusion of being a privileged voyeur, peeping in on a private world, separate from the rest of the audience.

Mulvey adds that cinema also develops scopophilia 'in its narcissistic aspect', exploiting the viewer's desire to identify with a human face and form that they recognize as being similar to their own (Mulvey 1989c: 17). Here, she refers to Lacan, who proposed that human identity or the ego is formed during the Mirror Stage, when an infant first encounters itself as a separate entity, typically through its reflection in a mirror. The infant joyfully identifies with its mirror image. However, this identification is based on an imaginary misrecognition because the mirror presents an *ideal* ego – perfect, complete, and in control – at odds with the infant's actual experience of its body, which is at this stage uncoordinated and helpless as well as speechless (Lacan 1993: 2). Human individuals are haunted by this idealized image of themselves throughout their lives.

It is not difficult to connect this to cinema. Sitting in the auditorium, fascinated by the images on the screen, the spectator's awareness of themself as a separate entity temporarily dissolves – forgetting who they are and the time and space they inhabit, they become like an infant, whose ego boundaries are yet to be formed. At the same time, the cinema re-evokes the moment at which their ego came into being. The spectator identifies with the glamorous stars on the screen – ego ideals who 'act out a complex process of likeness and difference' in an echo of the infant's misrecognition of itself as the Other in the mirror, who is more perfect, complete, and in control (Mulvey 1989c: 18).

The French film theorist Christian Metz likened the cinema screen to a mirror, in his 1975 article 'The Imaginary Signifier', published in

Screen. But although he, too, draws links between the Mirror Stage and cinematic perception, it is Mulvey's groundbreaking analysis that spells out the implications for cinema's organization of sexual difference: 'In a world ordered by sexual imbalance, pleasure in looking has been split between active/male and passive/female' (Mulvey 1989c: 19). She argues that there are two forms of looking involved in the spectator's relationship with the screen. One is active scopophilia, which uses another person as an erotic object and in which the subject's identity is different from and distanced from the object on the screen. The other arises from narcissism and the formation of the ego, where the spectator identifies with their on-screen likeness (Mulvey 1989c: 18).

In narrative cinema, woman plays a 'traditional exhibitionistic role' – her body is held up as a passive erotic object for the gaze of male spectators, so that they can project their fantasies on to her. She connotes '*to-be-looked-at-ness*' (Mulvey 1989c: 19). The men on screen, on the other hand, are agents of the look, with whom spectators identify to enjoy vicarious control and possession of the woman. We can see, in almost any classic Hollywood film, that the heroine is an object to be looked at: she is filmed in soft focus, 'coded for strong visual and erotic impact' (Mulvey 1989c: 19).

Narrative cinema, then, is not unlike other visual forms that display women as sexual objects, such as pin-ups or striptease. But what distinguishes cinema from other forms of female sexual display is that it incorporates permutations of the look into its very structure, predetermining how the woman is to be looked at, and thus placing all spectators in the 'masculinized' position of looking at her. Mulvey observes that there are three sets of looks involved in cinema: (1) the camera's look at the pro-filmic reality, (2) the audience's look at the final film product, and (3) the characters' looks at each other. The conventions of narrative cinema strive to make the audience forget the camera and the fact that they are watching a film. They work to deny both (1) and (2) in favour of (3) – all in the interests of creating a 'convincing' illusion of a world where the male protagonist acts as the spectator's surrogate (Mulvey 1989c: 26). In the narrative structure, too, the male drives the story forward, while the female has a passive role, linked to her status as spectacle. As well as identifying with 'the active power' of the hero's gaze at the woman, the spectator acquires the illusion of ordering and controlling the narrative themself (Mulvey 1989c: 20).

But, psychoanalytically speaking, woman poses a problem for the male who looks at her. Due to her 'lack' of a penis, woman evokes the unpleasurable threat of castration. This castration anxiety is related to the child's original trauma of discovering the mother does not have a penis; consequently, according to Freudian theory, the child assumes she is castrated. Films master this castration anxiety in two ways: first, by re-enacting the trauma through voyeurism, investigating the woman and revealing her guilt (i.e. her 'castration'), then either punishing or saving her; second, by disavowing castration through fetishism, i.e. endowing the woman's body with extreme aesthetic perfection, which diverts attention from her 'missing' penis and makes her reassuring rather than dangerous.

The voyeuristic strategy is typical of film noir, a genre known for its sexually alluring but deadly *femmes fatales*. In the process of investigating an intrigue or murder, the hero (usually a detective) ends up investigating *her*. The hero, who thus represents the Law, brings her crimes to light but, at an unconscious level, it is really the problem of her sexuality that is being resolved. Through his voyeuristic and sadistic control over her, the hero reaffirms his own mastery (and, by proxy, the male spectator's). *The Maltese Falcon* (1941) exemplifies this: it ends with the *femme fatale* being arrested, prison bar-like shadows cast across her as she is taken away in a caged lift.

Mulvey herself relates this strategy to Alfred Hitchcock's films. Technically, they do not belong to film noir, but they foreground voyeurism, putting the man on the right side of the Law, and woman on the wrong side. The protagonist of *Rear Window* (1954), for example, is a photojournalist, Jeffries (James Stewart), who has broken his leg in the line of professional duty and is confined to his flat where he spies on his neighbours through his window. The film clearly establishes his voyeurism and activity through his hazardous profession and the photographic equipment lying around the flat. At the same time, his accident, which immobilizes him in his seat, 'puts him squarely in the fantasy position of the cinema audience', who must also limit their activity to looking (Mulvey 1989c: 24). For most of the film, the audience is restricted to Jeffries's narrative and optical point of view. The window frame, for him, becomes like the cinema screen for the audience: a canvas onto which he projects his repressed desires and fantasies. Using binoculars and his long-lens camera to get a better view, he effectively becomes a 'Peeping Tom' – in fact his nurse Stella accuses him of being one.

Jeffries's girlfriend Lisa (Grace Kelly), a fashion model who is always flaunting her new clothes, is, according to Mulvey, an exemplary exhibitionist – typical of women in narrative cinema. However, Jeffries only becomes fascinated with Lisa when she crosses over from the space of the spectator to the opposite block, which corresponds to the space of the screen. Lisa climbs into a neighbour's apartment to find incriminating evidence of a murder and is surprised by the neighbour when he returns. Thereby, Jeffries is able to see her 'as a guilty intruder exposed by a dangerous man' who threatens to punish her (Mulvey 1989c: 23). This gives Jeffries the chance of saving her.

For Mulvey, Josef von Sternberg's films exemplify fetishism, especially those starring Marlene Dietrich, the fetishized female form *par excellence*. In its broadest meaning, fetishism disavows knowledge in favour of belief, conjuring up the superstitious beliefs of 'primitive' societies. It is a resonant concept for Mulvey, because – as she states in her later work *Fetishism and Curiosity* – it appears in the writings of both Marx and Freud; these thinkers used it to question the rationality of Western thought, which has supposedly overcome such beliefs (Mulvey 1996: 2). For both Marx and Freud, fetishism has to do with value or, more particularly, overvaluing. Marx discussed commodity fetishism to try to understand how abstract values come to be invested in things, and how their origins as products of labour or social relations are disavowed. Freud, on the other hand, in his 1927 essay on the topic, explored how fetishism 'ascribes excessive value to objects considered to be valueless by common consensus' (Mulvey 1996: 2).

The Freudian and Marxist conceptions of fetishism coalesce in Mulvey's discussion of the dream factory of cinema. On the cinema screen itself, the woman as erotic spectacle is the perfect fetish. The camera fetishistically isolates fragments of her body (face, breasts, legs) in close-ups. The use of such close-ups for the heroine stresses that, unlike the hero, she is valued above all for what her appearance connotes, for her beauty and sexual desirability. One is unlikely to find similar sorts of shots of the male hero, unless the shots concern narrative events; for example, in *Rear Window*, the camera focuses on Jeffries's broken leg. The close-ups of parts of the female body, on the other hand, have the quality of a 'cut-out or icon', temporarily halting the flow of the narrative to invite erotic contemplation and

FREUDIAN FETISHISM

Fetishism is now commonly understood in a sexual sense, as overvaluing part of a sexual object as a substitute for the whole. Specifically for Freud, fetishism defends against castration anxiety arising from the awareness of sexual difference. In his view, a child's initial knowledge of sexual difference rests on the absence or presence of the penis. Boys assume that everyone owns a penis until they discover that the mother does not have one; then they believe she must have been castrated. The fetishist, however, refuses to believe the woman is castrated. He uses the fetish to cover over and disavow the sight of her 'wound', overvaluing other, more harmless parts of her body. This disavowal is such that it allows the fetishist to retain his belief that the woman has a penis and simultaneously acknowledge that she doesn't.

Mulvey initially explored the topic of fetishism in her essay 'Fears, Fantasies and the Male Unconscious or, "You Don't Know What is Happening, Do You, Mr Jones?"' (1973), where she demonstrates that, far from being 'the private taste of an odd minority', as most people think it is, fetishism pervades the mass media, mostly at an unconscious level (Mulvey 1989b: 13). Considering sculptures by Allen Jones, who produced ideas for the milkbar in *A Clockwork Orange* (1971), she argues that Jones's work is valuable from a feminist perspective because it clearly conveys how male castration anxiety comes to be projected onto the female form, which is then appropriated as a fetish – for example, how woman is represented adorned with phallic shapes. We can see this in many media images of women, where certain 'well-known phallic extensions', such as guns, cigarettes, and high-heeled shoes 'divert the eye' (Mulvey 1989b: 8).

shattering the illusion of depth rather than enforcing verisimilitude (Mulvey 1989c: 20).

The fetishization of women in cinema extends to the cult of a female star such as Dietrich. Here, too, overvaluation implies a refusal to recognize sexual difference, making the female form 'safe' for the enjoyment of the male gaze. The glamour of the star is emphasized and becomes pleasurable in itself, 'a perfect streamlined image of femininity' (Mulvey 1996: 8). Mulvey argues that Sternberg's films represent a special instance in narrative cinema as they bypass the male protagonist's controlling gaze altogether, facilitating a 'direct rapport' between the image and the spectator (Mulvey 1989c: 22). The woman in these films, she writes, is 'a perfect product, whose body, stylised and fragmented by close-ups, is the content of the film and the direct recipient of the spectator's look'.

Mulvey emphasizes the need for women to understand the mechanisms of voyeurism and fetishism that underlie the patriarchal unconscious of narrative film. At the time of writing 'Visual Pleasure and Narrative Cinema', her aims were iconoclastic: to break the codes and destroy narrative pleasure. At the end of her essay she calls for filmmakers to 'free the look of the camera into its materiality in time and space and the look of the audience into dialectics and passionate detachment' (Mulvey 1989c: 26). At that point, she imagined a feminist cinema along the lines of radical modernist practice, with its strategies of self-reflexivity, disruption, and defamiliarization, as exemplified by Bertolt Brecht's work in theatre, on the one hand, and Jean-Luc Godard's post-1968 films (such as *British Sounds* [1970]) on the other. She also went on to make her own films, including *Riddles of the Sphinx* (1977) (in collaboration with Peter Wollen), which, with its 360 degree pans and voiceover commentary, puts these ideas into practice. However, her stance on film and the possibilities for feminist filmmaking has changed a lot since then, perhaps most dramatically in her recent book *Death 24 × a Second* (see Mulvey 2005: 190), which will be discussed briefly in the final chapter.

THE FEMALE SPECTATOR

There have been countless reactions to 'Visual Pleasure and Narrative Cinema', countering – or at least confronting – Mulvey's view that narrative cinema positions its spectators as male, catering only for male fantasies and pleasures. The essay exerted such a strong impact on the direction of feminist film theory that many subsequent works constitute a direct response to it. In particular, it was felt to ignore the circumstances of the female spectator – is she *always* constructed by the film-text in the same way as the male spectator? If she identifies with the look of the male protagonist, is she, too, impelled to make the female protagonist into an object of erotic desire? What about the 'actual' women in the audience?

Such debates became the hot topic of feminist film theory during the 1980s. Critics pointed to the tradition of the 'Woman's film' and other types of melodrama, especially from the 1930s and 1940s, to demonstrate that films that specifically try to address female spectators have always existed. Films such as *Stella Dallas* (1937), *Mildred Pierce* (1945), and *Letter from an Unknown Woman* (1948) centre on a female protagonist whose viewpoint appears to guide the film and deal with feminine concerns and experiences (see Gledhill 1987; Doane 1987; Kuhn 1994). However, the need to create mass entertainment for female audiences gave rise to an irreconcilable gap between the patriarchal ideology at work in these films and female desires expressed in them. The movies' endings typically strived to resolve these contradictions – for example, at the end of *Stella Dallas*, the heroine realizes that her desire to be 'something else besides a mother' conflicts with her maternal duty. At the same time, the film lays bare this contradiction and permits women's lived frustrations to find a voice.

Mulvey herself anticipated these concerns in her 1977 essay on Douglas Sirk's melodramas where she argues that 'having a female point of view dominating the narrative produces an excess which precludes satisfaction . . . Hollywood films made with a female audience in mind tell a story of contradiction, not of reconciliation' (Mulvey 1989e: 43). In her 'Afterthoughts on "Visual Pleasure and Narrative Cinema", inspired by *Duel in the Sun*' (1981), she reconsiders the role of the female spectator. Whereas before she had maintained that narrative cinema does not offer a place for female spectators, here she argues that the female spectator might enjoy the fantasy of control and freedom over the narrative world that identification with the hero affords and that she can cross the lines of gender in her identification with the male hero because her gender is itself divided.

At this point, Mulvey alludes to Freud, who identified a pre-Oedipal 'phallic phase' in girls (associated with activity), later repressed when they develop their femininity; during many women's lives, there are frequent regressions to this phallic phase, leading their behaviour to alternate between '"passive" femininity and regressive "masculinity"' (Mulvey 1989d: 35). It is this 'internal oscillation of desire' that lies dormant in the female spectator and awaits to 'be "pleasured"' in stories like *Duel in the Sun* (1946), a Western with a female protagonist, Pearl, who is torn between the path towards 'correct' femininity (becoming a 'lady'), and being a tomboy; these split desires are dramatized in the way she is caught between two men, Jesse and Lewt. Comparing the female spectator to Pearl, Mulvey argues that 'she temporarily accepts "masculinisation" in memory of her "active" phase', however, the film does not dramatize the success of masculine identification but its sadness. So, too, Mulvey suggests that the female spectator can identify with the active, masculine position, but this is a form of 'transvestite' identification that sits uneasily on her (Mulvey 1989d: 33).

The American feminist film theorist Mary Ann Doane has led debates on genres where the implied spectator is female and has expanded Mulvey's paradigm in several important ways. In 'Film and the Masquerade: Theorizing the Female Spectator' (1982), she defines the structure of the gaze in terms of proximity and distance in relation to the image rather than, as Mulvey put it, a distinction between 'male/ active' and 'female/passive' and the female spectator's 'transvestite' oscillation between these two forms of identification. The particular problem posed by the female spectator, Doane claims, lies in the fact that woman functions as the image, resulting in a potential failure of distance between spectator and screen. The female spectator has two options. The first is to over-identify with the woman on the screen, becoming emotionally over-involved with the heroine. The other option, equally 'untenable' from a feminist perspective, is for the female spectator to take the heroine as her own narcissistic object of desire (Doane 1991: 31). In both, the spectator loses herself in the image.

Doane suggests that a way out of this dilemma is for the female spectator to read the on-screen image of her likeness as a masquerade. The psychoanalyst Joan Rivière addressed the topic of masquerade in her essay 'Womanliness as a Masquerade' (1929). Reflecting on women who flaunt their femininity in an exaggerated way, she suggests that such behaviour is a masquerade or mask adopted by certain women 'to hide their possession of masculinity and to avert the reprisals expected if she was found to possess it . . . The reader may now ask how I define womanliness or where I draw the line between genuine womanliness and the "masquerade". My suggestion is . . . they are the same thing' (Rivière 1986: 38). Here, Rivière deduced the socially constructed character of femininity. Doane appropriates the notion of masquerade to theorize the possibility of creating a distance between the female spectator and woman as image, making the latter available for viewers to critique. As she recognizes, however, within films, female characters who masquerade are often punished – for instance, *femmes fatales* who try to usurp the masculine activity of looking, or horror film heroines whose terrified gaze is mastered by the monster's gaze.

Finally, Doane analyzes a photograph, '*Un Regard Oblique*' (1948) by Robert Doisneau, to illustrate the way Hollywood integrates the male gaze into its narratives and at the same time denies the female gaze. The photograph depicts a man and a woman looking at a shop window. The woman stands in the centre and the photograph appears to emphasize her look. However, the real power of the gaze lies with the man, who stands in the corner of the picture. His gaze, cutting across and effectively erasing the woman's gaze, is aimed at a painting of a female nude. Unlike the picture that captures the woman's attention, which is absent to the viewer, the painting of the nude is prominently displayed in the photograph. Therefore, despite her narrative centring, the female *subject* is overtaken by the picture as *object* of the male gaze; the photograph is, in effect, a 'joke' at her expense. For Doane, the photograph exemplifies the sexually differentiated structures of looking inscribed in cinema: 'The fetishistic representation of the nude female body, fully in view, insures a masculinization of the spectatorial position' (Doane 1991: 29).

Feminist film theorists have also undertaken research to discover more about actual audiences and how they respond to films. Instead of looking at what kind of spectator is 'implied' by films, these theorists engage in 'empirical' studies of actual, historical, or current audiences by looking at exhibition practices, forms of reception, and the social composition of audiences. Ien Ang's *Watching Dallas* (1985) pioneered this approach in television studies. In both film and television studies, the shift has been accompanied by the recognition that audiences do not just passively absorb pre-given meanings 'forced' upon them by media texts but actively create their own meanings. However, many feminist critics working with this approach tend to combine it with psychoanalytic theorizing (Hansen 2000). Despite the incontestable value of empirical research, theory has never outlived its uses. One reason for this is that empirical audience research – for example, in the form of interviews with real spectators – cannot by itself help us understand the often-unconscious desires motivating people to watch movies. Another is that the notion of the 'real audience' in empirical audience research, with its parameters defined by the researcher, is just as much a construct as the textual spectator (Brunsdon 1992: 125).

Attempts to give the concept of the female spectator a historical and ethnographic specificity also led feminist theorists to explore differences between women, particularly as shaped by different experiences of race, class, and sexuality. For example, studies have suggested that the 'look' of lesbian spectators of mainstream films can override the male viewpoint constructed in those films, enabling the films to be read pleasurably 'against the grain' (Ellsworth 1990). In 'White Privilege and Looking Relations: Race and Gender in Feminist Film Theory' (1988), Jane Gaines extends these concerns to race, providing a critique of feminist film theory's use of psychoanalysis. This type of analysis, she argues, may 'lock us into modes of analysis' based on a male/female opposition that supports mainly white middle-class values and prevents us from understanding the position of women who suffer other sorts of oppression (Gaines 2000: 340). She illustrates her case with an analysis of a film about a black fashion model, *Mahogany* (1975), starring Diana Ross, chosen because it is tempting to read its themes of sadism, voyeurism, and photography psychoanalytically, in the manner of Mulvey. Yet, to do this, Gaines points out, is to 'step into an ideological signifying trap set up by the chain of meanings that lead away from seeing the film in terms of racial conflict' (Gaines 2000: 344). She also points out that, unlike the white man, the black male character in *Mahogany* and black males in other mainstream American films do not have the power or privilege of sexual looking. This makes race a determining factor in the male gaze. In the US, this can historically be traced back to power relations between blacks and whites during slavery. Gaines highlights the need for a theory of black representation that is sensitive to history. bell hooks has also explored these particular issues in her book *Black Looks* (1992).

Meanwhile other critics, for example D.N. Rodowick, have found fault with the binary logic of Mulvey's argument. But while her insistent use of oppositions, such as male/female, active/passive, scopophilia/narcissism, is often attributed to her dependence on psychoanalysis, Rodowick points out that Freud himself 'problematizes any strict binary division between "maleness"/"femaleness" and activity/passivity' in questions of desire and identification (Rodowick 2000: 192). Such criticisms have, in turn, led to a more precise use of psychoanalysis by the feminist film theorists discussed in this book, who all engage with these debates at some level.

SUMMARY

In her celebrated essay 'Visual Pleasure and Narrative Cinema', Mulvey proposes that narrative cinema produces the male as agent of the look and the female as the object of spectacle through mechanisms of voyeurism and fetishism. In this way, narrative cinema imposes 'masculine' viewing strategies on all of its spectators, irrespective of their actual sex. Her argument gave rise to a number of debates, particularly as to whether narrative cinema systematically excludes women and the 'female gaze'. To answer these questions, feminist theorists investigated films targeted at female viewers as well as studying the actual reception of films by female audiences. Mulvey herself modified her arguments in her 'Afterthoughts' to her essay, where she considers the role of the female spectator. She argues that, in accepting the 'masculinized' subject position offered to her by narrative film, the female spectator can engage in a form of 'transvestite' identification, which involves alternating between genders. However, the universalizing tendencies of Mulvey's psychoanalytic framework also came under scrutiny, including from black feminist theorists, who stressed the importance of integrating the role of history into the analysis of filmic representation, as well as of recognizing that women's oppression is not exclusively determined by gender.

3

THE FEMALE VOICE

Do female artists, writers, and filmmakers express themselves differently from male artists? Does such a thing as 'the female voice' exist and, if so, is it possible to define it? These are questions that are highly relevant in the visual arts, especially cinema. Kaja Silverman explores the concept of the female voice in her book *The Acoustic Mirror* (1988), where she points out that the feminist critique of cinema has largely been confined to the image track, particularly – as we saw in Chapter 2 – to the ways in which woman is constructed as an object of the male gaze. Extending her analysis to the soundtrack, Silverman argues that 'classic' cinema is obsessed with the sounds produced by the female voice. Women's voices are invariably tied to bodily spectacle, presented as 'thick with body' – for example, crying, panting, or screaming – and insistently held to the rule of synchronization, which marries the voice with the image. But while women may scream, cry, prattle, or murmur sweetly in the course of any film, they have little or no authoritative voice in the narrative; their speech is characterized as 'unreliable, thwarted, or acquiescent' (Silverman 1990: 309). Silverman contrasts this with experimental feminist film practice, which strives to free the female voice from its incessant reference to the female body. However, her intention is not to set up a simple opposition between classical narrative and experimental or independent cinema – she emphasizes that even films that come under the classic narrative category can go beyond those 'classic' conventions (Silverman 1988: ix).

For Silverman, the concept of the voice refers in the first instance to the recorded voice of film soundtracks and the rest of this chapter, particularly the sections entitled 'Female Confessions' and 'Fantasies of the Maternal Voice', examines her analysis of how sexual difference is constructed through film soundtracks. It will show how Silverman draws on works of psychoanalysis, semiotics, film theory, and feminist theory to illuminate her field of study but also how she deconstructs her theoretical sources to reveal that some of them, including the writings of French feminist theorists Luce Irigaray and Julia Kristeva, unwittingly echo classic cinema's characterization of the female voice. The section on 'Female Authorship' will show how she expands her conceptualization of the voice to consider questions of authorial voice. Through a reappraisal of Roland Barthes's 'The Death of the Author', she insists on the importance of the authorial voice for feminist purposes and offers suggestions for 'finding' the female voice in the authorial systems of both classic narrative and independent cinema. This flexible concept of the voice enables her to express some of the main ideas that run through her work. On the one hand, *The Acoustic Mirror* is about the female voice and demonstrates Silverman's 'rewriting' of female subjectivity through a critical re-evaluation of semiotics and psychoanalysis. On the other, it also about male subjectivity and how it shores itself up against its own lack – a topic that Silverman explores further in her book *Male Subjectivity at the Margins* (1992), discussed in Chapter 7.

Silverman starts *The Acoustic Mirror* by questioning the psychoanalytic assumption that informs much film theory, namely, Freud's insistence on locating absence and lack at the moment of the child's discovery of sexual difference at the Oedipal stage. Following Lacan, Silverman contends that the child, of either sex, is already marked by absence and lack *before* its awareness of sexual difference. Its experience of lack first arises during the Mirror Stage, which occurs before the Oedipus Complex, when the infant is speechless (*infans* in Latin means 'speechless'), usually aged six to eighteen months.

Prior to the Mirror Stage, the child exists in undifferentiated oneness with the mother – a state of 'Imaginary plenitude' with no conception of difference or lack. At the Mirror Stage, it learns that a number of objects that it initially believed to belong to its own flesh – faeces,

THE SYMBOLIC, THE IMAGINARY, AND THE REAL

According to Lacan, these are the three 'orders' or 'registers' that structure our relationship with reality; they are not agencies of the mind, as in Freud's model of the ego, superego, and id, but more like multiple universes in which we simultaneously exist. While each is radically different from the others, the three orders overlap with each other at certain points. The Symbolic Order is the order of social Law, which depends upon language and is reproduced through 'the Name of the Father'. The Imaginary, on the other hand, is the realm of the image, creating the illusion of similarity and wholeness, where Self and Other blend into each other; it is the realm of dual relationships, including the early mother–infant relationship. Finally, the Real is that which is beyond language and which resists symbolization – particularly the body in its material aspect.

a comforting blanket, the mother's voice and breast – are actually separate. Lacan calls these 'part objects' *objets petits autres* ('objects with only a little "otherness"', cited in Silverman 1988: 7). Through this process of 'splitting' itself, the infant begins to apprehend itself and the external world of objects. The experience retrospectively acquires the significance of castration when the child enters the Oedipus Complex and acquires language. In Lacan's metaphorical reading of the Oedipus Complex, the taboo of incest is turned into a function of language: the father says 'no' to the child's incestuous desire for the mother. Lacan calls this 'the Name of the Father', identifying the father with the law. The Name-of-the-Father positions the infant as a subject in the Symbolic Order, the realm of language and social codes, characterized by absence and desire (activated by loss). Through this, the imaginary unity of mother and child is broken up forever.

By becoming subjects in the Symbolic Order, we are *all* constituted by lack or 'symbolic castration', according to Lacan. The social and linguistic order exists before us: it masters us, rather than us mastering it. From this Lacanian perspective, Silverman argues that Freud's determination to tie castration to the 'discovery' of sexual difference not only overlooks the child's earlier experiences of loss and lack but is motivated by a desire to distance the male subject from the idea of lack. Freud performs an act of displacement, which deposits lack at the site of the woman's body. A similar displacement occurs in films. While Mulvey argued that the male spectator's pleasure revolves around identifying the woman with lack and thereafter punishing or taming her, Silverman demonstrates that the female subject is made to bear the burden of a lack that properly belongs to both male and female subjects. To compensate for his own lack, which he cannot bear, the typical male subject projects it onto the female, so that he can sustain a fantasy of being unified and complete. Moreover, in film, not only is the woman's body constructed as lacking; so is her voice.

As a medium, cinema is perceptually very rich and offers an incredible illusion of life-like presence, an illusion to which sound greatly contributes. Like the child at the Mirror Stage, the audience joyfully possesses the sounds and images in their plenitude and disavows their actual absence. However, film theorists suggest that once we become conscious that the frame hides things from our hearing and gaze – once we become aware that someone else is controlling what we see and hear – feelings of lack and disempowerment overcome our pleasure. This someone else is cinema's invisible enunciator or 'speaking subject'; the film theorist Jean-Pierre Oudart calls it the 'Absent One' (Silverman 1988: 11).

Rather than specifying the director or scriptwriter as the enunciator, film theorists such as Oudart emphasize the Symbolic (i.e. the technological and ideological) machinery that structures what we hear and see. This includes the site of cinematic production that is veiled from us and to which we do not have any access. Theorists often call the camera – and, far less often, the tape recorder – the enunciator, but in fact the function of enunciator exceeds any one handling individual or one particular machine.

The enunciator bears the traits of a powerful symbolic father – knowledge, transcendental hearing and vision, self-sufficiency, and discursive power. The viewing subject now understands himself or herself to be lacking these traits (a form of symbolic castration). For Silverman, cinematic texts compensate for this lack through a sleight-of-hand whereby the gaze/audition that controls what we see/hear seems to be that of a fictional character rather than that of the camera/tape recorder. This operation is known as 'suture', a concept that Silverman introduces in her early writings, especially in *The Subject of Semiotics* (1983).

SUTURE

Suture literally means 'stitch'. Originally a psychoanalytic term used by Lacan's disciple Jacques-Alain Miller, suture has been adopted into film theory to describe the methods by which viewers are absorbed into the narrative and encouraged to identify with characters. Silverman is one of several theorists who have elaborated the theory of suture; others include Jean-Pierre Oudart, Daniel Dayan, and Stephen Heath. The technique of shot/reverse-shot has been identified as central to suture. This aligns the viewer's point-of-view with that of a character and urges him or her to want to see the next shot. For example, in one shot, we see a view of the sea; then, in reverse-shot, we are shown a fictional character whose point-of-view has supposedly determined the previous shot. Shot 1 has thus been converted into a signifier for Shot 2, linking the field of the 'Absent One' to a fictional character's gaze. Through this operation, viewers in the auditorium are 'stitched' into the subject-positions films construct for them. They are urged to identify with the gaze of the fictional character and to deny that he/she occupies a separate space; an imaginary unity is created between spectator and screen.

Heath and Silverman, however, have argued that the system of suture exceeds any particular shot formation and encompasses all the operations of classical narrative – including editing, lighting, camera movement, framing, and sound. These elements create narrative coherence through absence and lack, not only activating the viewer's desire for more narrative but also diverting attention from the level of enunciation to the level of fiction.

Through every frame-line and cut, cinema threatens the viewer with castration, making them aware of their own irredeemable lack by gesturing to the greater authority of the hidden enunciator. At the same time, this wound is sutured over with a signifying chain that distracts the viewer by offering meaning and narrative. Silverman suggests that this affects male more than female viewers, as the former are accustomed to denying their lack. Indeed, male subjectivity is formed through an imaginary or illusory identification with the phallus, which, in Lacan's view, is not equivalent to the penis but simply the emblem of positive values within the Symbolic Order; in patriarchal cultures, those values are identified with male power. If the male subject remembers his shortcomings, including his alienation from the origins of discourse and/or the site of production, that identification becomes troubled.

The healing of narrative can only happen after the wound has been inflicted; and the more wounded we are, the more desperate we become for meaning and narrative. We can see this at work in *Psycho* (1960), where we follow and identify with Marion Crane until she is murdered halfway through the film in the famous shower scene, where every cinematic cut appears to be the stab of a knife. This inflicts a traumatic wound on the viewer who is left with no-one to identify within the empty motel except the cinematic enunciator. So desperate is our need for meaning and narrative that we then identify with Marion's murderer, Norman Bates, when he arrives to dispose of her body and her belongings. We even feel anxious for him when, momentarily, Marion's car refuses to sink into the swamp. Suture is the 'hook' by which the film accomplishes this entrapment of the viewer (Silverman 1983: 212).

FEMALE CONFESSIONS

So far, the theory of suture has largely been discussed in terms of the visual image. What is the function of the voice in such identifications? For Silverman, the sound equivalent of shot/reverse-shot and other suture elements is the rule of synchronization, which matches image and sound frame by frame. Lip-synching, for example, establishes a smooth fit between body and voice. It gives the illusion that the image is speaking 'directly', without mediation from the whole machinery of production; it serves to 'stitch over' this intruding machinery and helps to immerse viewers in the fiction. In most auditoriums, sound speakers are placed next to the screen to enhance the illusion that the images are the source of the sounds and voices when, in fact, sound and images are produced separately; generally, sound is mixed after the images have been produced and often after they have been edited.

In classic narrative cinema, the voices of both men and women are synchronized with their bodies yet, Silverman argues, the rule of synchronization is more forcibly applied to women's voices. We can see this in the disparity of functions assigned to male and female voiceovers. The voiceover is an exception to the rule of synchronization. The audience hears it for the most part as a disembodied voice.

Generally, voiceovers inhabit a slightly different temporal or spatial location from that in the diegesis. For example, in the film noir *Double Indemnity* (1944), the hero speaks into an office tape recorder, while past events are visualized for the audience in extended flashback.

The voiceover of *Double Indemnity* is actually an embodied voiceover, as the character to whom it belongs appears on-screen. Embodied voiceovers tend to be linked with characters marred by trauma, who are speaking from extreme situations; the voiceovers in *Double Indemnity* and *Sunset Boulevard* (1950) belong to a dying man and a dead man, respectively. These voiceovers are autobiographical and confessional, with the extended flashback revealing how the speaker arrived at his present state. The male variety of embodied voiceover is generally restricted to 1940s film noir and its contemporary revivals.

Female voiceovers, if they occur, have similar characteristics to the embodied male voiceover of film noir – for example, *Mildred Pierce* (1945), itself a hybrid of melodrama and film noir, and *Letter from an Unknown Woman* (1948), where the female speaker utters her story in the form of a confessional letter. Silverman argues that classic narrative of cinema has no female voiceovers comparable to the disembodied male voiceovers, which narrate from a privileged perspective 'outside' the diegesis in films such as Orson Welles's *The Magnificent Ambersons* (1942). She identifies one exception, *A Letter to Three Wives* (1949) which, according to her, is the only Hollywood film in history to feature a disembodied female voiceover. However, it is an exception

DIEGESIS

A term designating elements belonging inside the fictive narrative world, often used in connection with film sound. Film sound is said to be 'diegetic' when its source is represented as being in the story-world: for example, the characters' dialogue (including voice-off), the sounds of objects in the story, music coming from instruments or recording equipment within the story. Voice-off (not to be confused with voiceover) is diegetic because it occurs when a fictional character is heard off-screen while still occupying the space of the diegesis, even though his or her voice is not at that point synchronized with his or her image. 'Non-diegetic' sound, on the other hand, comes from a source outside the story: for example, added soundtracks or voiceover.

that proves the norm. Although the character never fully appears on-screen, her voiceover is 'curiously corporealized' (Silverman 1988: 49). Her appearance is frequently talked about by the other characters, who study her photograph, 'obliquely angled so as to resist and tantalize our vision'.

In classic cinema, a voice has power and privilege to the extent that it has no bodily complement in the image. Just think of *The Wizard of Oz* (1939), where everyone quakes before 'the great and powerful Oz' speaking in voice-off until Dorothy's dog Toto reveals him to be just a little old man hiding behind a curtain. The moment such a voice is synchronized with its speaker's moving lips it loses its power. It is true that, even in its male form, disembodied voiceover (as opposed to voice-off) is rare in narrative cinema – except in French New Wave films, although Silverman does not address this in *The Acoustic Mirror* – and is much more common in documentary. For Silverman, the phenomenon nonetheless epitomizes the overall pattern through which sexual difference is constructed in soundtracks: at its logical extreme, classic cinema pits the disembodied male voice against the synchronized female voice. With its omniscient vision and audition, the disembodied voiceover speaks with utmost authority; its voice is that of the Law. It has the transcendental properties of the enunciator – significantly, the narrator of *The Magnificent Ambersons* identifies himself as Orson Welles, the film's director, at its close.

Generally, however, Hollywood prefers to suture its viewers through fictional male characters within the diegesis whose *synchronized* voices possess similar attributes to the disembodied voiceover. This involves reinventing the interior level of narrative and the exterior level of enunciation as different areas within the narrative. It consigns the woman to a safe place 'inside' the diegesis where she can be overseen and overheard, while the man is situated in a framing space 'outside', where he can identify with the functions of transcendental vision, hearing and speech associated with the enunciator or disembodied narrator. So, just as, on the visual register, men are aligned with seeing and women with being seen, so, on the auditory register, men hear and women are overheard.

One strategy by which narrative cinema accomplishes this is by containing the female voice in a letter, a song-and-dance performance, or a film-within-a-film. In *A Letter from an Unknown Woman*, the female voice is contained in the interior of the narrative through a letter from

Lisa (Joan Fontaine) to Stefan (Louis Jourdan). As Stefan reads, Lisa comes to life as an embodied voiceover, existing only through his consciousness; she is already dead by the time he comes to read the letter. In another strategy, the female voice is associated with involuntary utterance. The involuntary utterance Hollywood tries most to extract from woman is the scream. Meanwhile, a third strategy ascribes 'linguistic incapacity' to the woman – giving her voice an accent, speech impediment, or an idiosyncratic flavour, which serves to fix the voice to the body and also lessens its discursive authority (Silverman 1988: 61). In *Singin' in the Rain* (1952), silent-screen star Lina Lamont (Jean Hagen) is told: 'You're a beautiful woman; audiences think you have a voice to match'. Yet when Lina speaks she does so 'shrilly and ungrammatically, with a heavy Bronx accent' (Silverman 1988: 45). Her voice is precisely what causes problems when her studio decides to make talking pictures; it refuses to be regulated by the diction coach.

When recording, Lina initially cannot be heard as she does not speak into the mike, hidden in a bush. The sound engineer then tucks the mike into her bosom; now her body – her heartbeat and her pearl necklace, which rattles when she moves – drowns out her voice! At the preview screening, the audience jeers at Lina's performance precisely because the sounds she makes are so 'embodied', at times inordinately loud, constantly fluctuating depending on her distance from the mike. At a crucial point, the soundtrack goes out of synch with the picture, making the male villain speak with her voice while she speaks with his. The rule of synchronization is temporarily violated for comic effect – mainly to humiliate Lina.

After the disastrous preview, her co-star Don (Gene Kelly) and his friend Cosmo decide to turn the film into a musical with Don's sweetheart Kathy (Debbie Reynolds) dubbing Lina's voice. Both women's voices are constructed as deviant, treacherous, and unreliable: while Lina is presented as a cunning fraud, stealing another's voice so she can continue her screen career, Kathy's voice has deviated from its 'natural' bodily origins, attaching itself to another.

FANTASIES OF THE MATERNAL VOICE

Hollywood's visual and sound regimes place the male subject on the side of symbolic Law and discursive authority. So, too, do many readings of Lacanian theory. The infant takes up its place in the Symbolic

Order by accepting the Law of the Father and repressing its desire for the mother's body. As Mulvey puts it, this leaves the mother to 'either . . . give way to the word, the name of the father and the law, or else struggle to keep her child down with her in the half-light of the imaginary' (Mulvey 1989c: 15). To enter the Symbolic Order is to enter a masculine realm where women's relationship to the laws of language and society is defined as marginal.

This has led a number of feminist theorists to locate the source of a repressed feminine language or voice in the pre-Oedipal mother's body. In particular, the girl's pre-Oedipal relationship with her mother has been singled out for defining the specificity of both the female voice and female sexuality. In Kristeva's work, the feminine is linked to the semiotic, a feature of language that exists beneath Symbolic logic and grammar. It draws its sustenance from the *chora*, a term meaning 'receptacle' or 'enclosure', which Kristeva borrows from Plato and identifies with the womb. The *chora* evokes an image of unity between mother and child, prior to the Mirror Stage and the Symbolic Order. It flows with pre-linguistic elements, like the pulsations of the primitive drives, and resurges wherever discourse collapses – a revolutionary force against the Name-of-the-Father. Kristeva celebrates the 'homosexual' union of mother and daughter in the *chora*, although she denies that 'homosexual' here means 'homo*sexual*', disavowing the erotic aspect of that union.

In *The Acoustic Mirror*, Silverman provides a critique of Kristeva's ideas. Kristeva removes the mother as far as she can from the dominant social and linguistic order so that she can define a place from which to challenge it but, in doing so, she unwittingly partakes in a wider 'refusal to assign the female voice a viable place within the symbolic' (Silverman 1988: 105). Her association of the semiotic and the maternal with the pre-linguistic is, Silverman argues, 'in no way threatening to sexual difference as it is presently constituted' (Silverman 1988:102). Kristeva implies that the semiotic is a position that can be taken up irrespective of gender, thus appearing to resist reducing the feminine voice to a biological essence. However, all the writers she cites are male, including Joyce and Mallarmé. For Silverman this is an evitable outcome of Kristeva's theory: 'For Kristeva, to speak is thus necessarily to occupy a "male" position; even the maternal voice can be heard only through the male voice', so of course her conception of the artist is male (Silverman 1988:113).

Such fantasies of the maternal voice, which psychoanalytic theory shares with cinema, are at odds with the crucial role the mother plays in introducing the infant to language and culture. An infant usually distinguishes its mother's voice before other voices. It hears her even before it can see her. The theorist Guy Rosolato has proposed that the maternal voice creates an 'acoustic envelope' or blanket of sound around the child, functioning as an 'acoustic mirror' in which it finds its own voice and identity. Despite the symbolic mastery the mother exerts in the child's infancy as its first teacher, storyteller, and commentator on the world, many cultural fantasies appear to reverse the positions of mother and child, stripping her of her linguistic authority. In Kristeva's theory, the infant is ejected from the *chora,* enabling the mother to be placed inside. In cinema, the female subject is also effectively asked to occupy the position of the newborn baby whenever she is identified with noise, babble, or the cry – especially in horror films, where she is reduced to situations of utmost helplessness and dependency, voiced through verbal and auditory incompetence.

According to Silverman, the maternal voice in cinema serves as an 'acoustic mirror in which the male subject hears all the repudiated elements of his infantile babble' (1988: 81). The maternal voice is at times viewed in a positive light, as a symbol of bliss and plenitude, but at other times sinisterly, as a symbol of impotence and entrapment. For Silverman, both attitudes are exemplified in Francis Ford Coppola's *The Conversation* (1974), which follows a surveillance expert Harry Caul (Gene Hackman) who is obsessed with overhearing others, yet adamant not to be overheard himself. He prefers always to be 'outside the door', as his girlfriend puts it – that is, in a position of exteriority which, together with his formidable surveillance equipment, affords him the illusion of discursive mastery, knowledge, and power; as we have seen, these are also the phallic traits attributed to the cinematic enunciator.

When Harry records a conversation in San Francisco's Union Square, involving a young woman, Ann, talking with her lover Paul, he appears to be concerned only with obtaining 'a big fat recording' for his client, Ann's husband. He does this by selecting the best tracks and remixing the recording dialogue in order to make every word audible, including Paul's utterance, 'He'd kill us if he had the chance'. However, Harry is clearly fascinated by other parts of the conversation, which he replays repeatedly. He is irresistibly drawn to Ann's maternal voice as she sings a children's song and remarks, of a derelict on a park bench, 'He was once somebody's baby boy'. Her words evoke 'the lost comfort and security of childhood' and make Harry yearn to be wrapped up in the soothing blanket of the maternal voice (Silverman 1988: 90).

Later, Harry goes to the hotel where the couple are to rendezvous in Room 773, ostensibly to prevent a murder but really so he can eavesdrop, drilling a hole in the wall in which he places a microphone. From Room 773, he hears a scream, which he thinks is Ann's. It later transpires that it is not Ann but her husband who was intended all along as the murder victim, lending Paul's words a meaning hitherto unforeseen by Harry, 'He'd kill us if he had the chance'. For Silverman, the scream – part human, part electronic – which Harry hears emanates from his own psyche. The female voice functions as an acoustic mirror allowing him to displace his own impotence. Yet it also reminds him of it, making him hide under the bedclothes, curling up like a foetus. Harry's surname is 'Caul', a word for the 'inner membrane enclosing the foetus before birth', which later becomes afterbirth. 'Caul' signifies Harry's fantasy of regaining wholeness and plenitude through a return to the womb (being enclosed in the pure sonorousness of the female voice) but also his desire to shed that dependency, gain control over sound, and maintain a position 'outside' the maternal enclosure. In the latter instance, the female voice functions as something that defiles and must be ejected.

THE 'HOMOSEXUAL-MATERNAL FANTASMATIC'

French feminist theorists such as Kristeva and Irigaray consistently associate feminine speech and writing with the body, particularly the maternal body. This has laid these theorists open to charges of reducing femininity to the body. In the light of Silverman's findings in *The Acoustic Mirror*, this notion of *écriture féminine* ('feminine writing') is doubly problematic, as Hollywood cinema also ties the female voice to the body. It is, she suggests, equally at odds with experimental feminist film practice, which detaches the female voice from the female body, using the strategy of multiple or disembodied voiceovers. In films such Mulvey's *Riddles of the Sphinx* (1977), Sally Potter's *Thriller* (1979) and *Gold Diggers* (1983), Yvonne Rainer's *Film About a Woman Who* (1974), and Marguerite Duras's *India Song* (1975), voices go in and out of synchronization, at times issuing from visible sources on-screen, at others speaking over the images, making it difficult to anchor voices to specific bodies. Disembodying the female voice is seen as liberating in these films as it is primarily as a body, surveyed by the male gaze, that woman is constructed in classic cinematic narrative.

According to Silverman, none has solidified the connections between the female voice and the body more than Irigaray. In *This Sex Which is Not One* (1977), Irigaray tries to describe the different economy of female desire in terms of the female form. Unlike the male organ, the female sex is not 'one' but several – with vulval lips that are always touching each other. Her vision of feminine language hangs on this model of multiplicity, contiguity, and simultaneity, valorizing the sense of touch over sight. Irigaray claims a woman speaks by wandering off in numerous directions, 'touching upon' rather than focusing, appearing mad or incoherent 'from the standpoint of reason' (cited in Silverman 1988: 144). Silverman comments: 'many of Irigaray's formulations of "the feminine" are completely consonant with traditional derogations of woman, such as the claim that she is irrational, speaks incoherently, can't concentrate on one thing at a time, lacks visual authority, is closer to her body, or is more oriented towards pleasure than man' (Silverman 1988: 148). She acknowledges that there is indeed a culturally repressed dimension of femininity but refuses to locate it in such criteria or in the female body. The thrust of her critique is not to jettison the body from the feminist project – she recognizes that 'rewriting the body' is vital, but believes that it should be undertaken in order to change the ways in which women discursively relate to their bodies (Silverman 1988:146).

Silverman's alternative model of female subjectivity situates maternal identification within the Symbolic Order. This enables us, she claims, 'to speak about a desire which challenges dominance from within representation and meaning, rather than from the place of a mutely resistant biology or sexual "essence"' (Silverman 1988:124). This also forms a contrast to Kristeva's idea of a de-eroticized pre-Oedipal mother–child union, which simply acts as a disruptive force to the Symbolic. Silverman calls her theoretical alternative the 'homosexual-maternal fantasmatic', drawing on the libidinal resources of the so called 'negative' Oedipus Complex (Silverman 1988: 125).

The Oedipus Complex presents a particular problem for the girl, not least because the mother is her first love-object. It demands that she switch her allegiance to the father; by learning to desire him, she acquires the cultural role of femininity. Yet she remains torn between desire for the mother and desire for the father for the rest of her life. Thus Freud put forward a theory of the 'negative' Oedipus Complex, where the child loves the parent of the same sex; it is 'negative' in the sense that the girl's erotic leanings towards her mother (and the boy's towards his father) are considered socially inadmissible. Freud's female followers such as Jeanne Lampl-de Groot specified that in these instances the girl refuses to change her love-object from mother to father, laying the basis for homosexual orientation in later life.

In Silverman's account, the negative Oedipus Complex teems with subversive political potential, for there the girl does not learn the socially constructed feminine role of passivity. Silverman makes the negative Oedipus Complex the site of the daughter's identification and desire for the mother, which speaks against the traditional desire for the father. This desire can manifest directly in lesbian sexuality or more diffusely in forms of female bonding. Either way, Silverman's idea of the 'homosexual-maternal fantasmatic' is offered as a revisionary founding fantasy for feminism, figuring both women's unity and their occasionally necessary separation from men (Silverman 1988: 125).

FEMALE AUTHORSHIP

Although, as Silverman writes, 'the voice cannot speak without assuming an identification, entering into desire, or evoking the Other' (Silverman 1988: 162), in terms of cinematic authorship, the female voice is hampered by a number of other factors – including unequal opportunities in the film industry. A film's creative vision is usually attributed to the director and most well-known directors are men. However, women have always worked behind the scenes, often without being credited. Not surprisingly, feminist theorists are often sceptical about the concept of authorship, particularly in relation to Hollywood. The authorial system of the majority of Hollywood films excludes the female voice. Their complex machinery of enunciation, moreover, militates against construing any film as the voice of its 'author' (Silverman 1988: 209).

The critical impact of Barthes's 'The Death of the Author' has caused the idea of authorship to be further questioned. In this 1968 essay, Barthes challenged the central position occupied by the author as origin and owner of the text's meaning, claiming that texts are created through the impersonal force of language or discourse rather than through the author's personal choice. He removed the biographical author as the transcendent source of the text's meaning 'outside' the text – and relocated him or her 'inside' the text so that the author is *produced by* the text instead of being its origin. With the death of the author, Barthes proclaimed the birth of the reader, liberated by the author releasing his or her hold over the text's reception and meaning.

In Silverman's view, Barthes announces the death of a specifically male-defined idea of the author. Nonetheless, within theoretical discourse, his arguments have generated an indifference towards who is speaking – which is just as uncongenial to the search for the female authorial voice as male-biased notions of authorship. Film theory has since put an emphasis on *film* as discourse, banishing the author from textual analysis. Henceforth the question of 'who or what is speaking' has generally been translated as 'who or what is looking' – identifying the camera, more than any other part of the cinematic apparatus, as the enunciator. In tandem with the shift from author to reader, analysis has moved to how subjectivity is constructed in the text *for* the spectator.

Although she has no wish to restore the author as the transcendent source of meaning, Silverman asserts that it *does* matter who is speaking. Not crediting women filmmakers with authorship obviously deprives them of their voice and authority, and also starves recognition of some of the ways in which female subjectivity is inscribed in cinema. Silverman salvages the notion of the director as author and suggests he or she may be regarded as '*one* of the speakers of his or her films' (Silverman 1988: 202). As she does not wish to dispense with the biographical author altogether, she subtly indicates that the author 'outside' the film is articulated through the author 'inside' the film.

For example, the author may appear in the film, either as a voice or as an image, as in Hitchcock's cameos. Such appearances should not be read as transparently embodying the author 'outside' the text but as the authorial subject constructing itself within the film, often in an idealized identification with the text's point of origin. The author as a discursive construct also includes the interviews and other publicity around his or her films. Although Silverman obviously does not mention this in her 1988 book, the DVD era has given us yet another form of authorial self-manufacture – the director's voiceover commentary that can be activated while viewing a film.

Alternatively, the director may identify with a fictional character who 'stands in' for him or her. This identification may go across gender lines, as it does for Italian director Liliana Cavani, who has a strong identification with her male characters. However, wherever it occurs, this desire for cross-gender identification has to be 'read in relation to the biological gender of the biographical author, since it is clearly not the same thing, socially or politically, for a woman to speak with a female voice as it is for a man to do so, and vice versa' (Silverman 1988: 217). Finally, authorial citation may take the form of 'a formal or narrative "image"' (Silverman 1988:215). What gives a director's body of work its 'libidinal coherence' is 'the text "inside" the author', or what psychoanalysts Jean Laplanche and J-B. Pontalis call 'the fantasmatic', the unconscious fantasy or group of fantasies that structure one's life as a whole, shaping one's dreams, objects of desire and identifications. These may revolve around the Oedipal fantasies identified by Freud but are not determined solely by them, for the fantasmatic is 'constantly drawing in new material', remaining open to new influences from the outside world (1988: 216). Again, Silverman's example is Cavani, whose films repeatedly return to the scene of undressing; for example, in *Francesco* (1989), she relates the story of Francis of Assisi, who renounced his power, wealth, and privilege to help the needy, literally becoming naked in one scene. Silverman reads this investment in forms of male subjectivity that say 'no' to power as the sign of what she regards as Cavani's feminist authorship.

SUMMARY

This chapter has focused on the concept of the female voice in Kaja Silverman's *The Acoustic Mirror*. Silverman argues that women's voices in classic narrative cinema are invariably tied to the spectacle of their bodies, held more forcibly to the rule of synchronization than male voices are. For example, female voiceovers never narrate from a disembodied, omniscient perspective 'outside' the diegesis as some male voiceovers do. Silverman contends that the female voice in cinema functions as an acoustic mirror containing elements repudiated from male subjectivity. She also takes issue with French feminist theorists, such as Irigaray and Kristeva, who identify the female or maternal body as the source of a pre-Symbolic repressed feminine language, whereas Silverman herself strives to locate the female voice within the Symbolic Order. She puts forward an alternative model of female subjectivity in her theory of the 'homosexual-maternal fantasmatic' and outlines strategies for a theory of female authorship.

4

TECHNOLOGIES
OF GENDER

In her landmark essay 'The Technology of Gender' published in 1987, Teresa de Lauretis radically re-thinks the concept of sexual difference. Up to this point, feminist theory had largely conceived sexual difference in binary, ahistorical, and heterosexist terms – as the difference between 'Man' and 'Woman'. De Lauretis sought instead to articulate the social and sexual differences to be found *among* or *within* women. Although she utilizes the tools of semiotics and psychoanalysis, she is critical of those discourses, as she is of the male bias of the work of philosopher and cultural historian Michel Foucault. However, it is precisely her turn to Foucault in 'The Technology of Gender' that enables her to accomplish what she claims existing psychoanalytic feminism was unable to do, namely, to address the fraught and paradoxical relationship between *women* – as historically specific individuals – and *Woman* – an imaginary cultural representation.

This chapter focuses on the concerns de Lauretis discusses in her books *Alice Doesn't* (1984) and *Technologies of Gender* (1987), while the next chapter will be devoted to her other book *The Practice of Love* (1994). These chapters do not intend to give a chronological overview, but instead to show how she constantly re-visions her ongoing concerns by exploring them through different sets of literary or filmic texts and theoretical frameworks. For example, although the 'technology of gender' is a concept that she sets out around the middle of her career, it is one that revisits and reformulates earlier ideas from *Alice Doesn't*, just as it anticipates aspects of *The Practice of Love*, which again reworks the idea.

De Lauretis herself describes the movement of her work in a similar way when, in *Technologies of Gender*, she comments that this book represents a development from *Alice Doesn't* with its awareness that feminism, besides being a 'rereading' of our culture's master-narratives, is also a 'radical rewriting' of them (de Lauretis 1987: xi). Such rewriting 'inscribes the presence of a different, and gendered, social subject'. This aptly characterizes de Lauretis's own use of male theorists such as Foucault and Freud, whose work she rewrites in unorthodox ways. Uncovering unexpected alliances with her feminist project and similarities between these apparently disparate thinkers, her own work becomes a feminist 'remake' of theirs. In a slightly later article, 'Guerrilla in the Midst: Women's Cinema in the 80s' (1990), she applies a similar strategy, which effectively dismantles ready-made oppositions between avant-garde and mainstream cinema and suggests the mobility of women's desire and agency even within so-called mainstream vehicles. All this firmly places de Lauretis's work within a new phase of feminist film theory starting during the 1980s, which seeks to reclaim female agency within dominant discourses rather than merely viewing those discourses as oppressive.

BEYOND THE PARADOX OF WOMAN

> Over and over . . . she meets the image of Woman in books written by men. She finds a terror and a dream, she finds a beautiful pale face, she finds La Belle Dame Sans Merci, she finds Juliet or Tess or Salomé but precisely what she does not find is that absorbed, drudging, puzzled, sometimes inspired creature, herself, who sits at a desk trying to put words together.
>
> (Cited in de Lauretis 1989: 34n5)

This excerpt from Adrienne Rich's essay, 'When We Dead Awaken: Writing as Re-Vision' (1971), neatly sums up the way in which women are simultaneously absent and present in dominant culture. It is this paradox, de Lauretis remarks, that has been feminist thinkers' first task to unravel – the paradox of woman as 'constantly spoken of' while she herself remains 'inaudible', 'displayed as spectacle and yet unrepresented' (de Lauretis 1989: 26). She, however, points out that this paradox is in fact 'grounded in a real contradiction'. Women – as real social beings – are not the same as 'the Woman', yet they are 'caught', experientially and conceptually, between the two. This is what happens to women on an everyday level, bombarded as they are with cultural fantasies of the 'Woman' in media and advertising, and expected to live up to those images.

The problem is encapsulated in the Italian director Federico Fellini's film *Giulietta degli spiriti/Juliet of the Spirits* (1965), which de Lauretis analyzes in *Technologies of Gender*. Juliet is a housewife whose husband barely pays any attention to her and whispers the name of his mistress, a fashion model, in his sleep. Although a fictional character, Juliet can be said to figure women as real social beings; she is also played by Fellini's wife, Giulietta Masina, who is a well-known actress in her own right and, to some extent, we expect the film to be autobiographical. On the other hand, Juliet's 'pretty neighbour', a high-class prostitute named Susy (Sandra Milo) embodies the image of Woman, Juliet's glamorous and desirable Other. Early on, a clairvoyant tells Juliet that she can fix her problem by making herself more attractive to her husband. Later, hallucinatory voices – the titular 'spirits' – instruct Juliet to follow Susy. In fact, two of Juliet's spirits look just like Susy (they, too, are played by Milo). The two women are pointedly contrasted – Juliet is dwarfed by Susy's/the spirit's taller and more shapely figure and struggles to keep up.

In another recurring hallucination, Juliet sees a girl burning on a rack, martyring herself to preserve her virginity – a key motif in the Italian Catholic image repertoire. Juliet is caught in a hall of mirrors reflecting conflicting cultural representations of Woman both as virgin and whore – images that are 'incessantly held up, suggested, or exhibited to her by her culture, her family, her religion, and her fantasies' (de Lauretis 1987: 100). Juliet is trapped in the contradiction between women and Woman. The image of Woman, moreover, casts none other than Man's shadow. In Juliet's fantasies one can see images that recur obsessively throughout Fellini's work: her 'spirits' are his more than they are hers (de Lauretis 1987: 104).

For de Lauretis, it is imperative for film analysis to address the non-coincidence between women as historically-specific individuals and 'the Woman' produced by dominant discourses. When she writes 'Woman' (usually with a capital 'W'), she means 'a fictional construct', an essence ascribed to all women distilled from numerous dominant Western cultural discourses (de Lauretis 1984: 5). Very often the notion of

'Woman' is an attempt to contain women within ideas of femininity, enigma, proper womanhood, nature or evil. By contrast, the term 'women' designates 'the real historical beings who cannot as yet be defined outside of those discursive formations, but whose material existence is nonetheless certain' (de Lauretis 1984: 5). Now, in their attempt to render the absent present, feminist theories of sexual difference have tended to focus on women's difference from men; they have, for instance, identified affirmative instances of women's difference through notions of women's culture, mothering, *écriture féminine*, and femininity (see, for example, the discussion of Irigaray and Kristeva in Chapter 3). But – according to de Lauretis – this traps feminist thinking within a conceptual opposition between man and woman, which is already embedded within patriarchal society and its discourses (de Lauretis 1987: 1). It merely produces universalized concepts of man and woman, or makes woman represent difference itself, again universalized: Woman as Other from Man. Once again, woman figures as an 'archetypal essence', preventing the possibility of speaking of differences among or within women (de Lauretis 1987: 2). Therefore, in such feminist discourses, as well as in patriarchal discourses, real historical women, who are engendered differently in terms of their experience of class, race, and sexual relations, are simply conflated with 'the Woman'.

De Lauretis's aim is precisely to articulate this more specific form of gendered subjectivity and for that, she asserts, 'we need a notion of gender which is not so bound up with sexual difference as to be virtually coterminous with it' (de Lauretis 1987: 2). If the term sexual difference has restricted feminist theory within the conceptual binary of 'Man' and 'Woman', then so has psychoanalysis itself. Psychoanalysis always defines woman in relation to man, usually conceiving her within the same terms of reference. De Lauretis states: 'That is why psychoanalysis does not address, cannot address, the complex and contradictory relation of women to Woman, which it instead defines as a simple equation women = Woman = Mother' (de Lauretis 1987: 20). This, she emphasizes throughout her work, is 'one of the most deeply rooted effects of the ideology of gender' and, to address it, she turns to Foucault's theories.

THE TECHNOLOGY OF SEX

In works such as *Discipline and Punish: The Birth of the Prison* (1975) (a history of forms of punishment) and the three-volume *The History of*

Sexuality, Foucault offers an analysis of how power is exercised in society through a network of forces and institutions. Unlike his mentor, the Marxist theorist Althusser, Foucault focuses on local forms of power, rather than state apparatuses such as the government or police. By historicizing forms of knowledge and power, he shows that existing power-systems are not inevitable or fixed, but can be resisted or changed. A key Foucauldian term is 'discourse', roughly meaning a 'power-system'. For Foucault, power operates through discourses and there are a number of power discourses in society, internalized by individuals, and shaping their reality.

In *The History of Sexuality: Vol. 1*, first published in 1976, Foucault overturns the received wisdom that sexuality is a 'natural' and private matter, arguing that sexuality is discursively constructed in culture. He also refutes the 'repressive hypothesis' – shared by psychoanalysis and popular belief – that the culture of the last three centuries has driven sexuality underground (Foucault 1998: 10). On the contrary, religious, scientific, and legal institutions have made sexuality an object of their power-knowledge, seeking to extract 'the truth' about sex. In so doing, they have not constrained sexuality but rather caused a proliferation of sexual discourses; they have enabled diverse sexual behaviours to be identified and flourish.

Underpinning Foucault's theory of sexuality is a conception of power that is *not* repressive, not laying down limits and taboos, and refusing sex and pleasure. That, he argues, is the old concept of power as the law, which is exerted in a hierarchical fashion, and historically embodied in the absolute monarch or medieval feudal lord. By contrast, he conceives power as both pervasive and *productive* – of sexualities, pleasures, knowledges, and practices. Power is neither positive nor negative. It incorporates resistance: 'where there is power, there is resistance' (Foucault 1998: 95). Power comes 'from below' and 'from innumerable points' (1998: 94). Resistances exist at every point in the power network.

Foucault offers us a notion of a 'technology of sex' (1998: 90), defined as a set of techniques or regulated procedures that 'produce sex and the desire for sex as their end result' (de Lauretis 1984: 86). In Foucault's terminology, technologies are discourses of power. Technologies of sex construct sexuality through discourses that support state interests. For example, since the eighteenth century, techniques such as medicine, pedagogy, demographics, and economics have

implemented state-sanctioned discourses about four 'objects of knowledge': (1) children's sexuality, (2) women's bodies, (3) the fertility
of couples, and (4) sexual deviancy (Foucault 1998: 105). These
discourses, in effect, 'implanted' these objects of knowledge into individuals, families, and institutions. Their effect was 'to produce the
subject as a sexual subject according to culturally specified categories
such as male or female, normal or deviant, healthy or pathological,
heterosexual or homosexual, and so forth' (de Lauretis 1994: 286).

THE TECHNOLOGY OF GENDER

Foucault has been criticized for not distinguishing between the positive and the oppressive effects of power (de Lauretis 1987: 18). De
Lauretis also believes that Foucault does not sufficiently recognize that
technologies of sex solicit men and women differently. Nevertheless,
she uses Foucault's theory of technologies and discourses of power to
resituate gender within a wider network of power relations. Just as
Foucault argues of sexuality, so de Lauretis says gender is not an innate
element within human beings but the complex product of social technologies. Highlighting his silence on gendered subjectivity, she calls
the social technologies involved in the construction of gender 'technologies of gender'.

De Lauretis prefers the term 'gender' to 'sexual difference' because
it better conveys the ongoing process of social construction. In her
view, gender represents a *relation of belonging*, assigning individuals
positions *within* particular 'classes' or social groups and *relative to* other
classes or groups; it is gender, not sexual difference, that brings to the
fore the heterogeneity in men and women's experience of material conditions constituted as they are by multiple different relations to culture,
race, and class (de Lauretis 1987: 3–4). Talking about the social technologies of gender enables one to examine men and women in relation
to various power strategies, not merely in relation to each other.

The social construction of gender even occurs at the ordinary level
of filling in a form: there are boxes marked *M* and *F* for us to tick.
Most women are likely to tick the *F* box automatically, that is, they
will officially represent themselves as women (if any men choose to
tick the F box, that would have entirely different connotations). The
women think that they are marking the *F* on the form, but the *F* in
fact is marking itself on them – sticking to them 'like a wet silk dress'

(de Lauretis 1987: 12). We can see the social construction of gender in what Althusser called 'ideological state apparatuses' – the media, schools, family, and law courts. All these institutions produce discourses that have the power to produce and promote representations of gender, which are then accepted and internalized by subjects. Not least among these technologies of gender is cinema.

De Lauretis (rephrasing Althusser) describes gender as an 'ideologico-technological production' whose function is to constitute 'concrete individuals as men and women' (de Lauretis 1987: 6, 21). However, unlike Althusser and more like Foucault, she believes that agency and self-determination are possible at the level of subjective and micropolitical, day-to-day practices. The representation of gender by powerful social technologies such as mainstream cinema undoubtedly affects the way in which gender is internalized and constructed by individuals – but our individual self-representations of gender impact on the broader social construction of gender, too (de Lauretis 1987: 9).

Thus, in addition to the media, schools, law courts, and the family, de Lauretis discusses practices that exist within the margins of hegemonic discourses. For radical theories and avant-garde practices within the academy and the intellectual community – including feminism – are also technologies of gender. Inscribed within these micropolitical practices lie *the terms of a different construction of gender* (de Lauretis 1987: 18). Feminism and other radical theories and practices can intervene in the social process of gender (re-)construction, reworking and producing their own gender representations. At the local, subjective level or level of self-representation, they form a resistance to dominant representations.

Having arrived at this point, de Lauretis can now reformulate the stance, first articulated in her earlier work *Alice Doesn't*, that 'the constant slippage between Woman as representation . . . and women as historical beings' is driven by the contradictory logic of our culture in which women occupy a position that is both inside and outside of the ideology of gender. For, as well as being an 'effect of representation', gender is also the 'untheorized experience of women', capable of rupturing ideology precisely because it is unacknowledged by its spaces of representation (de Lauretis 1987: 119). To describe how women move in and out of gender as an ideological representation, de Lauretis uses a filmic analogy: the 'space-off', a term that designates space which cannot be seen within the frame yet which can be inferred from it. In mainstream cinema, space-off is usually concealed by editing techniques such as shot/reverse-shot, whereas avant-garde cinema gestures to space-off, either by commenting on its absence, or by alluding to the camera or spectator, both of whom occupy the field of the space-off. In de Lauretis's analogy, the male-centred representation of Woman inhabits the space of the frame, while women remain outside. The ongoing project of feminism, she says, is to define a view from 'elsewhere' – the elsewhere of current cultural discourse – from the blind spots or space-off of its spaces of representation.

RETHINKING WOMEN'S CINEMA

> When I look at the movies, film theorists try to tell me that the gaze is male, the camera eye is masculine, and so my look is also not a woman's. But I don't believe them anymore, because now I think I know what it is to look at a film as a woman.
>
> (de Lauretis 1987: 113)

'Women's cinema' can be defined in a number of ways – as films by women, made for women, or dealing with women, or all of these combined. Along with the Hollywood variety, *Juliet of the Spirits* is the kind of women's film that ostensibly deals with women's concerns. In her essay 'Rethinking Women's Cinema', de Lauretis reconceptualizes women's cinema as cinema made by and for women. Such cinema addresses the viewer 'as *a* woman' rather than as Woman (de Lauretis 1987: 142). Women's cinema 'defines all points of identification (with character, image, camera) as female, feminine, or feminist' (de Lauretis 1987: 133). In de Lauretis's view, this structure of address is far more important than considerations about whether women are being portrayed positively or not.

In another essay from *Technologies of Gender*, 'Strategies of Coherence', which focuses on the work of experimental feminist filmmaker Yvonne Rainer, she suggests that this conscious attempt to address the viewer as female, irrespective of its viewers' actual gender, is what 'allows the film to draw into its discursive texture something of that "Real" which is the untheorized experience of women' (de Lauretis 1987: 119). Women's cinema shows women as social subjects. It does this by recognizing differences among women – the various conjunctures of gender with race, class, age, and sexuality. As another example, de Lauretis offers Lizzie Borden's *Born in Flames* (1983), a film that depicts women from different classes and subcultures joining forces in a feminist revolt, not by setting aside their differences but precisely by acknowledging them – and thereby addressing its spectators as 'female in gender and multiple and heterogeneous in race and class' (de Lauretis 1987: 144). This is not to say that the film invites a one-to-one identification on the basis of the spectator's own particular identity (with black women off-screen identifying with black women on-screen etc.) but rather that the film enables more complex sorts of identifications to be formed and women's identities to be considered in their multiple socio-historical specificities.

However, de Lauretis also suggests that, in addition to the look, one may discuss women's cinema in terms of its narrative strategies. Narrative is a key technology of gender. Feminists and other radical practitioners and theorists have been known to be suspicious of it, associating it with the closure of false ideological endings. For example, early feminist cinema eschewed narrative in favour of formal experimentation. But, as spectators and also as filmmakers, women are equally drawn to narrative. Filmmakers who once avoided narrative have later turned to it, as Rainer did in *Film About a Woman Who* (1974). De Lauretis points out that closure is only a contingent feature of narrative, particular to certain forms such as classical Hollywood. More important to her is the fact that narrative is a mechanism of coherence – that is, a mechanism of meaning. She advocates the strategic deployment of narrative in order to 'construct other forms of coherence, to shift the terms of representation, to produce the conditions of the representability of another – and gendered – social subject' (de Lauretis 1987: 109).

In the essays collected in *Technologies of Gender* the term 'women's cinema' refers largely to avant-garde practice by directors like Rainer and Chantal Akerman. In her later essay 'Guerrilla in the Midst', de Lauretis considers a number of mainstream US films and offers a different view, asking the question can women's cinema 'still function as an alternative practice'? (de Lauretis 1990: 7). Her answer, an affirmative one, offers a new conception of women's cinema that cuts across the boundaries of independent and mainstream, avant-garde and narrative cinema – one that does not always privilege avant-garde and independent productions:

What I would call alternative films in women's cinema are those which engage the current problems, the real issues, the things actually at stake in feminist communities on a local scale, and which, although informed by a global perspective, do not assume or aim at a universal, multinational audience, but address a particular one in its specific history of struggles and emergency.

(de Lauretis 1990: 17)

The project of this guerrilla cinema is '*to work with and against narrative*', a theme that she first treated in *Alice Doesn't* (de Lauretis 1990: 9).

DESIRE IN NARRATIVE

In *Morphology of the Folktale* (1928), the Russian folklorist Vladimir Propp (1895–1970) explored the form of folktales around the world, arguing that every folktale is a variation upon a fixed repertoire of functions and roles. He identified seven roles that can be played by different characters but always serving the same narrative purpose (hero, villain, donor, helper, princess, princess's father, and dispatcher) and thirty-one functions that develop the narrative in any tale, such as 'the hero leaves home or sets out on a quest', 'faces a difficult task', and 'is married and ascends the throne'. Although all roles and functions do not appear in every tale, no tale can be told without drawing on them.

Propp's schema provided an influential model for structuralist narratologists, who have asserted that the myth of Oedipus underlies Western narrative. In *Alice Doesn't*, de Lauretis makes a similar claim that narrative structures are governed by Oedipal desire but unlike many others she does not view this as a universal 'given' but as the result of specific socio-historic circumstances that placed the Oedipus myth in narrative. In this, she follows Propp's lesser-known work, 'Oedipus in the Light of Folklore', where he suggests that the Oedipus myth embodies a broader social transition: from matrilinear patriarchy to direct patrilineal inheritance. In the earlier social order, power was handed down from the king to his son-in-law via marriage with the king's daughter, the princess. In the later order, which superseded it, power was directly transferred from the king to his son, intimating that the new king killed the old and producing the new folkloric theme of patricide. The Oedipus myth figures that traumatic transition, with aspects of the old era commingling within the new. For example, the role of the princess, who 'poses a difficult task or enigma [to the hero]' has been reduced to the sphinx's role as the monster who stands in the hero's path when he arrives at Thebes (cited in de Lauretis 1984: 115). The sphinx is the space that he must cross; he overcomes her by solving her riddle: 'What speaks with one voice, walks on four legs in the morning, on two legs at noon and on three legs in the evening and is weakest when it has the most?' Oedipus answers: 'Man'. As his reward, the people of Thebes make him king and offer him the queen's hand in marriage.

De Lauretis relates these Oedipal structures to mainstream narrative film. So many films follow an Oedipal trajectory, usually figuring a male hero-individual, who embarks upon a journey that will involve him crossing a boundary and penetrating 'the other space' (de Lauretis 1984: 119). This hero is 'the active principle of culture'. Woman is depicted as the object of his desire or the obstacle to be traversed, culturally coded as 'an element of plot-space, a topos, a resistance, matrix and matter' (de Lauretis 1984: 119). In the narrative trajectory of a typical Hollywood romance, for example, an active masculine subject conquers a reluctant or hesitant feminine object. Numerous narratives take the form of an investigation or a riddle to be solved. They are structured by a male desire, for it is Woman who represents the narrative enigma – think of the *femme fatale* of film noir. In the Oedipus myth, where it is the sphinx who gives Oedipus the riddle, we never find out what happens to the sphinx after the riddle is solved – only that she self-destructs. Like Freud's own inquiry into the 'riddle' of femininity, the question is posed *for* men, motivated by their desire *to know*. After all, Oedipus's answer to the riddle is 'man'; he says nothing about women. Even if the question is about what Woman most desires, women are not allowed to ask the question themselves or to articulate their own desires.

Instead, Woman is positioned as the space at the end of the hero's journey where, like Sleeping Beauty in the fairytale, she awaits him; he settles down with her and lives 'happily ever after' (de Lauretis 1984: 133). That the female subject is the figure of narrative closure confirms the male Oedipal trajectory of such narratives: the Oedipus Complex concludes for the little boy when he accepts the father's authority with the promise that he will one day assume his father's place with someone just like his mother. The Oedipal contract, therefore, lays the foundations for (patriarchal) social stability by urging the boy to identify with the father and objectify the mother.

Nonetheless, de Lauretis argues that narrative and visual pleasure should not be merely seen as belonging to dominant codes and fulfilling their oppressive functions. In cinema, identification takes place along three registers – that of the look, narrative, and sound. When these are explored altogether, it is possible to find a space for female desire and identification. Here, de Lauretis refers to the female Oedipal trajectory. Like the boy, a girl's first love is her mother. Freud characterizes the pre-Oedipal stage as the little girl's 'masculine phase'. This is due to the active aim of her libido, in contrast to the passivity she develops when she is initiated into femininity during the Oedipus Complex. Faced with the social or instinctual demands of heterosexuality, the girl surrenders her desire for the mother but, unconsciously or not, the desire stays active, leading to a bisexual disposition and a fluctuating pattern of (masculine and feminine) identifications and object-choices in later life. All this makes the passive 'feminine' identity sanctioned by patriarchy unstable and difficult to achieve.

De Lauretis believes that this 'sexual differentiation' within spectators challenges Mulvey's and other film theorists' definition of cinematic identification as masculine: 'The analogy that links identification-with-the-look to masculinity and identification-with-the-image to femininity breaks down precisely when we think of a spectator alternating between the two' (de Lauretis 1984: 142–3). She proposes an either/or model of cinematic identification, in which the female spectator benefits from a double desiring position. She claims there are two sets of identification, only one of which is already recognized by film theory. In addition to 'the masculine, active identification with the gaze (the looks of the camera and of the male characters) and the passive, feminine identification with the image', there exists another form of identification, which involves 'the double identification with the figure of narrative movement, the mythical subject, and with the figure of narrative closure, the narrative image' (de Lauretis 1984: 144). This double figural narrative identification is what anchors the subject in the narrative flow – it is also what allows the female spectator to occupy both active and passive positions of desire at once – she is a doubly desiring spectator whose desire is simultaneously 'desire for the other, and desire to be desired by the other' (de Lauretis 1984: 143).

The female Oedipal trajectory is rarely represented in cinema. However, one classic genre in which it regularly features is the commercial women's film, designed to attract female audiences through an ostensibly female narrative point of view. For example, in *Rebecca* (1940) the heroine appears to be the anonymous character played by Joan Fontaine, who alternates between the two positions of desire defining the female Oedipus Complex: desire for the father – Maxim DeWinter, who becomes her husband – and desire for the mother – Rebecca, the former Mrs DeWinter, now dead, who functions both as her rival and self-image. Her identification with Rebecca's image is implied in the portrait of the ancestor, whose costume she copies for a ball, and in the numerous items with Rebecca's initials scattered throughout the *mise en scène*.

Rebecca's beauty, wit, and breeding embody the image of Woman. But this image does not only figure as an object of desire for men. More crucially, it marks 'the place and object of a female active desire' – not only the heroine's but also that of the housekeeper, Mrs Danvers, who adored Rebecca and is jealous of the heroine who takes her place (de Lauretis 1984: 152). The portrait of Rebecca is not just there to display the image to which the viewer must aspire, according to the ideological procedure that reduces all women to 'the Woman'. Rather, 'the film narrative works precisely to problematize, to engage and disengage, the heroine's – and through her the spectator's – identification with that single image' (de Lauretis 1984: 153). Although enchanting, Rebecca is revealed as a duplicitous woman; and the heroine discovers that Maxim did not love Rebecca – he hated her.

The film thus gives expression to female desire but because, as de Lauretis puts it, 'cinema works for Oedipus', the heroine must kill off Rebecca/the mother and marry the father, ending her oscillation between 'femininity' and 'masculinity' and cancelling her desire for the female on behalf of the male. The heroine, like Freud's little girl in the Oedipal scenario, must give up her desire for Rebecca (and for that other evil surrogate mother, Mrs Danvers) and turn towards her father, who will make a woman out of her, by recognizing her femininity (or her castration). This is the process through which the little girl – and the female spectator – is forced to consent and be seduced into femininity. *Rebecca* has a conventional Oedipal resolution: Maxim returns to his estate Mandalay to find Mrs Danvers has gone up in flames and his heroine – now a mature woman, no longer a 'child' as he once called her – waiting for him. What is at stake here is not merely the image of Woman, but her *narrative* image. If Oedipus were to find that she was no longer there at the end of his journey, he would only try to find another. This is what Maxim does in seeking a replacement for Rebecca – another Mrs DeWinter, who will be more 'true' to him.

Patriarchal ideology cannot permit women to sustain their double desire and so, whenever that double desire is unwittingly registered in mainstream film, it must be presented as impossible or duplicitous, leading to a conflict that is resolved by the woman's destruction or reterritorialization – at the end of the film, she either dies or gets married. In her later book *The Practice of Love*, de Lauretis contrasts this with avant-garde/independent women's films where the heroine does not die or get married but escapes with another woman, who is not her rival, but her lover. In *Alice Doesn't*, however, de Lauretis claims that it is the task of feminist cinema to foreground rather than resolve the duplicity of the doubly-desiring woman. She calls for a disruption to the way in which narrative, meaning, and pleasure are constructed from Oedipus's point of view. This does not mean being anti-Oedipal, but being 'Oedipal with a vengeance', emphasizing the specific contradiction of the female subject within that scenario (de Lauretis 1984: 157).

SUMMARY

This chapter has focused on how de Lauretis addresses the contradictions arising between women as historical subjects and Woman as cultural representation. By adapting Foucault's theories to consider gender as a product of diverse social power relations, de Lauretis steers a course through the theoretical impasse affecting much feminist film theory of the 1970s and 1980s resulting from its reliance on the psychoanalytic concept of sexual difference, which tends to oppose 'Man' to 'Woman' in a universalizing fashion. Her concept of the technology of gender allows her to distinguish between women engendered differently by their specific socio-historical situations from the abstract formulation, 'Woman'. In her explorations, she provides a radical re-writing as well as a re-reading of dominant theoretical and narrative discourse. By arguing that feminism and theories of gender are also technologies of gender, she maps the possibility of a different gender construction through a view from 'elsewhere' that includes the 'untheorized experience of women', a blindspot of current cultural discourse. She also identifies working with and against narrative as a feminist filmmaking strategy, one that emphasizes the female subject's doubly desiring position.

5

QUEERING DESIRE

Even to this day, the term 'queer' raises a number of questions for those who hear it. Who or what is 'queer'? Is being lesbian or gay the same as being 'queer'? Can 'straight' people ever be 'queer'? The dictionary definition gives 'eccentric' as well as 'homosexual' and it is in this spirit of questioning what is 'normal', unsettling existing complacencies, and highlighting the dynamic and unpredictable nature of desire that Teresa de Lauretis coined the phrase 'queer theory' for the title of a conference at the University of California, Santa Cruz, in 1990. She also guest-edited the 'Queer Theory' issue of the journal *Differences*, which appeared a year later. Her work of the 1980s and 1990s laid many of the foundations of the field of queer studies, contributing to debates on lesbian spectatorship as well as offering a thoroughgoing critique of the heterosexist assumptions of most feminist theorizing on film. This chapter focuses on the exceptionally detailed theory of lesbian desire articulated in her book *The Practice of Love*, showing its power to illuminate lesbian films and cultural practices and situating this within the context of her other contributions to 'queer theory'.

'Queer' was once a derogatory, homophobic word; its victims reclaimed it as a term of self-empowerment in the late 1980s. In today's queer theory, especially that which follows the work of another gender theorist Judith Butler (b. 1956), it is an 'umbrella' term for the diverse range of lesbian, bisexual, gay, and transgender (L-B-G-T) behaviours, identities, and cultures. The common alliance between these positions was given a real urgency by the late 1980s AIDS crisis in the West and the accompanying tide of homophobia affecting queers of all sexes.

In coining the phrase 'queer theory', de Lauretis called for the dominant paradigms of homosexuality to be questioned and rethought, including clinical and other institutional discourses that frame it as an unnatural deviation from reproductive heterosexuality as well as popular media discourses that suggest that gay and lesbian sexualities are 'just another, optional "life style"' (de Lauretis 1991a: iii). She hoped to build on the newly-formed political alliance to facilitate discussion of modern gay and lesbian sexualities as emergent 'social and cultural forms in their own right', constituted in disparate socio-historical contexts, through multiple differences of race, gender, generation, and class. A coalition built on identification and difference across sex and gender lines, queer theory promised a critical dialogue enabling 'a better understanding of the specificity and partiality of our respective histories, as well as the stakes of some common struggles' (de Lauretis 1991a: xi).

In this context 'queer' was intended to displace old labels, including 'homosexual' (rejected by many lesbians and gays as a 'clinical' or derogatory term) and the phase 'lesbian and gay' which, although it implies differences by coupling the two terms, in common usage glosses over them. Queer theory also departed from the assumption in lesbian and gay criticism that the particularities of gay or lesbian experience result in gay or lesbian writers or directors expressing that outlook in their texts. Instead, queer theory emphasizes the social construction of lesbian and gay sexualities. De Lauretis herself prefers to speak of lesbian representation rather than lesbian expression, arguing that lesbian desire is not a property possessed by people 'predefined' as lesbians that is subsequently expressed in their art.

Queer theory's interrogation of essentialist, universal, or transhistorical notions of sexual 'identity' is inspired by poststructuralist ideas, especially Foucault's *The History of Sexuality*. In this book, Foucault argued that the modern epoch's investigations into the 'truth' of sex through medical, legal, and other discourses have initiated the multiplication and proliferation of sexual identities; the incitement to discourse has aroused rather than repressed sexuality, strengthening diversity by implanting 'perversions' into individuals (Foucault 1998: 37). 'Homosexuality', for instance, was invented as a category by nineteenth-century medical discourse, first recorded in an 1870 German article (Foucault 1998: 43). The term 'homosexual' designated a sexual *identity*, replacing what was formerly known as a series of *acts* (sodomy). According to this view, homosexuality is a category of knowledge, discursively constructed in society, rather than a fixed reality.

It is often said that Queen Victoria thought that there was no need to make lesbianism illegal because she didn't believe it existed. In fact, Foucault also overlooks the social construction of female homosexuality in favour of male homosexuality (he himself was a gay man). Lesbian representation has, historically, been associated with invisibility, partly due to the invisibility to which women's culture, more generally, is prone – one of the significant differences between gay male and lesbian culture, which de Lauretis intended queer theory to address.

In today's postmodern media, however, these issues of (in)visibility have shifted. Film producers have realized the commercial potential of 'lesbian chic' and its ability to crossover to mainstream audiences. Compared to the dearth of representation earlier, since the 1980s there has been a veritable explosion of lesbians on film – *Desert Hearts* (1985), *Go Fish* (1994), *Heavenly Creatures* (1994), *Bound* (1996), and *Mulholland Drive* (2001), to name but a few. *Ellen* (1994–98), *Tipping the Velvet* (2002), *The L-Word* (2004), and *Sugar Rush* (2005) testify to a comparable upsurge of television interest. Concerns have been voiced that this kind of lesbian visibility serves the purposes of heterosexual male titillation. De Lauretis does not argue that it necessarily does but that, by circulating the figure of the lesbian as a commodity, postmodern culture heightens lesbian visibility at the risk of blurring lesbian specificity – it appears to turn lesbian desire into a desire just like any other.

In terms of gay and lesbian equality rights, this might seem progressive. Nonetheless, de Lauretis and other queer theorists would argue that such a move reduces lesbian desire to the 'incidental, private, and thus . . . politically inconsequential' (Pick 2004: 109). Theorizing the social and sexual specificity of lesbian desire, on the other hand, underlines its personal, political, and public consequence.

FILM AND THE VISIBLE

> We're trying to construct a representation that is not simply one using the
> dominant codes ... I think we're trying to develop, whether as women critics
> or film- and video-makers, representations that are simultaneously decon-
> structions of dominant codes.
>
> (de Lauretis 1991b: 281)

In *Desert Hearts*, a college professor Vivian Bell (Helen Shaver) travels
for a quick divorce to Reno, Nevada, where she meets and is seduced
by the openly lesbian Cay Rivers (Patricia Charbonneau). Set in the
1950s, the movie utilizes the iconography of the Western in its land-
scapes and characterization, introducing Cay as having inherited her
father's 'wild streak' and driving backwards in her convertible at
60mph on the highway. Now a lesbian classic, the film was indepen-
dently produced and directed by Donna Deitch, then selected for
distribution by the Hollywood studio MGM.

Desert Hearts is, in de Lauretis's view, more 'honorable' than other
films that merely exploit the lesbian fad – after all, it 'declares itself
a lesbian's film' and that suggests a social responsibility on Deitch's
part (de Lauretis 1994: 114). However, de Lauretis points out, by
using 'lawful narrative genres', such as the romance and the Western,
its love story is just like any other (de Lauretis 1994: 122). Even
though the love is between two women, it leaves intact the heterosexual assumptions of the Oedipal narrative structure that she described
in her book *Alice Doesn't*, where an active masculine subject pursues
and overcomes a hesitant feminine object (see Chapter 4). Together
with 'its seamless narrative space, conventional casting and characterization', *Desert Hearts* – according to de Lauretis – simply transposes
lesbianism into Hollywood conventions without re-signifying those
conventions in any way (de Lauretis 1994: 114).

Lesbian spectators, however, might (and do) gain pleasure from
viewing a woman take the man's place as the active pursuer of a
romance. They are also adept at reading films subversively, 'against
the grain'. Elizabeth Ellsworth's study of audience reactions to the
Hollywood movie *Personal Best* (1982), which features a lesbian relationship between two athletes and is filmed in the usual voyeuristic
style, provides a good instance. While press-book pre-readings and
mainstream media reviews trivialized the film's lesbian relationship in

favour of its heterosexual romance, lesbian reviewers devised their own interpretive strategies enabling them to resist these dominant, preferred readings. They totally rewrote the film to make the lesbian relationship central, refusing to take the heterosexist ending on its own terms, imagining an alternative ending where the women reunite (Ellsworth 1990: 193).

The problem with this strategy of reading against the grain is that, like Deitch's approach to narrative in *Desert Hearts*, it does not create the conditions for another – and different – kind of visibility. As we have seen in the last chapters, what is conventionally constructed as visible within the field of audio-visual representation, and within cinema as a social technology in particular, is the female body held up to the male gaze. His gaze alone bears the power to signify desire, while the woman is either a narrative enigma to be 'pursued, investigated, found guilty or redeemed by man' or possessed 'as fetish object of his secret identification' (de Lauretis 1994: 112–13). Hence, de Lauretis signals the need for films to represent lesbianism in ways that alter these standard frameworks and *recreate* the conventions of seeing:

> Simply casting two women in a standard pornographic scenario or in the standard frame of romance, and repackaging them as a commodity purportedly produced for lesbians, does not seem to me sufficient to disrupt, subvert, or resist the straight representational and social norms by which 'homosexuality is nothing but heterosexuality' – nor *a fortiori* sufficient to shed light on the specific difference that constitutes a lesbian subjectivity.
>
> (de Lauretis 1994: 114)

The point is not just to make the invisible visible but, rather, to manoeuvre between different regimes of visibility. This, de Lauretis believes, is what Sheila McLaughlin's film *She Must Be Seeing Things* (1987) accomplishes: its originality lies in 'foregrounding that frame of reference, making it visible, and at the same time shifting it, moving it aside, as it were, enough to let us see through the gap' and 'to create a space for questioning . . . what *we* see in the film' (de Lauretis 1994: 113). Moreover, instead of negating lesbian desire by adapting it to conventional narrative romance, the film places itself 'historically and politically in the contemporary North American lesbian community' (de Lauretis 1994: 122). A similar argument could be made for another independent film, Rose Troche's *Go Fish*, which also portrays a North

American lesbian community in its social and sexual specificity. Despite its girl-seeks-girl romantic comedy premise, it slices up the linear flow of the narrative romance with interludes in which characters comment on its progress, enabling the audience, too, to cast a defamiliarizing glance at its standard frames of reference, creating the possibility of seeing differently or otherwise.

SEXUAL INDIFFERENCE

In her essay, 'Compulsory Heterosexuality and Lesbian Existence' (written in 1978 and first published in 1980), the lesbian poet Adrienne Rich used the term 'compulsory heterosexuality' to describe hetero-sexuality as an institution that oppresses women. She refers to numer-ous pressures that have, through the ages, either covertly socialized women or directly forced them to channel their sexuality into marriage and heterosexual romance, ranging from pre-capitalist daughter-bartering to post-industrial economics, from 'the silences of literature' to television images (Rich 1983: 144–5). Speaking specifically about desire, de Lauretis believes that heterosexuality 'is doubly enforced on women' – first, 'in the sense that women can and must feel sexually in relation to men', and second 'in the sense that sexual desire belongs to the other' (de Lauretis 1994: 111). In cultural representation, women often signify sexuality, but they tend to do so *for* men; rarely are they depicted as having their own sexual desires. In this standard way of looking, a woman's feelings towards another woman cannot be sexual, 'unless it be a "masculinization," a usurpation or an imita-tion of man's desire'. Freud himself is guilty of perpetuating such a view for, according to him, an active libido can only be masculine. In the orthodox psychoanalytic interpretation, lesbian desire is construed in terms of a 'masculinity complex'.

To describe this indifferent attitude to lesbian specificity, de Lauretis borrows the term 'sexual indifference' from Luce Irigaray. Within the regime of sexual indifference, there is only 'a single practice and representation of the sexual', one in which, according to Irigaray in her book *This Sex Which is Not One*, '*the feminine occurs only within models and laws devised by male subjects*. Which implies that there are not really two sexes, but only one' (cited in de Lauretis 2000: 385). In such a regime, a woman's desire for another woman simply appears incom-prehensible.

As her example, Irigaray cites Freud's studies of female homosexuality which, in her view, are really studies of male sexuality, as they interpret lesbians' desire for other women as basically a masculine desire. She puns on *homme* (French for 'man') and *homo* (Latin for 'the same') to create her neologism for this phenomenon of sexual indifference – *hom(m)osexuality* – which, de Lauretis also stresses, is a far cry from real homosexuality, i.e. lesbian and gay sexualities. Both male and female homosexuality are significantly different from heterosexual male sexuality and cannot be circumscribed by the latter's logic.

Lesbianism holds a primary attraction for feminism because it appears to reclaim for women a specifically female desire, autonomous from men; it means being the active subject of desire, of one's own desire, rather than the desire to be desired (by men). However, de Lauretis thinks that, like dominant discourses, feminist discourse also frequently glosses over the real sexual difference – that is, the psycho-socio-sexual difference – that lesbianism entails. Most feminist discourse tends to discuss lesbianism metaphorically, as a trope for an idealized all-female community. One form which that takes is what de Lauretis calls 'the homosexual-maternal metaphor', which describes the mother–daughter bond in 'homosexual' terms, instances of which have been discussed in Chapter 3.

De Lauretis views the centrality of maternal imagery as a dangerously conservative strain within feminism, especially at a time of anti-feminist backlash (de Lauretis 1994: 198). By attributing an erotic role to the mother, who stands for what all women have in common, such feminist discourses reduce female sexuality to maternity, resulting in the well-worn (and chauvinist) formula: women = Woman = Mother. In particular, de Lauretis criticizes Silverman's homosexual-maternal fantasy, where 'homosexual' – as Silverman borrows the term from Kristeva – really refers to homo*social*, woman-to-woman relationships. It reveals a tendency in feminist writing to sweep lesbian desire and sexuality 'under the rug of sisterhood, female friendship, and . . . the mother-daughter bond' (de Lauretis 1994: 116, 185).

In fact, Adrienne Rich set the precedent for this in 'Compulsory Heterosexuality and Lesbian Existence'. In order to counter the heterosexual institutions that characterize lesbians as deviant, she tried to emphasize that being a lesbian is both a normal and desirable choice for women. She coined the phrase 'lesbian continuum' to encompass a range of expressions of love between women, underlining the commonalities between lesbian and heterosexual women. Yet, for de Lauretis and many others, Rich enlarges the notion of lesbian existence so much that she erases lesbian specificity, allowing popular interpretations of her essay to read 'lesbian' as the more general term 'woman'. Here, the meaning of 'lesbian' has been converted into woman-identification, implying women who may or may not sleep together; and, if they do sleep together, it apparently makes no difference.

In this respect, de Lauretis's thought is more in tune with Monique Wittig, another of her influences, who made the controversial state-ment in her essay 'The Straight Mind' (1980) that 'lesbians are not women' (Wittig 1992: 32). De Lauretis read Wittig's work in the 1980s and it prompted her to write lesbian theory, as distinct from feminist theory. Wittig presents a concept of 'lesbian' that exists outside the gender system where woman is defined in relation to man. While de Beauvoir had written: 'One is not *born* rather one *becomes* a woman', Wittig asserts: 'one is not born *a woman*', turning the empha-sis from *born* to *woman* thus undermining the heterosexual definition of woman as 'the second sex'. For her, a lesbian's refusal to become or stay heterosexual is 'the refusal of the economic, ideological, and polit-ical power of man' (Wittig 1992: 13). It is in this economic and political sense that she means a lesbian is not a woman and advocates the dis-appearance of women as a class. In short, for Wittig, and also for de Lauretis, a lesbian is not merely someone with a particular 'sexual pref-erence', but a mode of being in the world that creates social and sexual autonomy from men.

De Lauretis consequently reveals the possibility of a different kind of female subject – an 'eccentric subject', eccentric in the sense that it doesn't 'center itself in the institution of heterosexuality', in which even feminism had been complicit (de Lauretis 2003). As mentioned in Chapter 4, de Lauretis has reconceptualized the notion of sexual difference. No longer merely the difference between Man and Woman, in her interpretation, sexual difference consists of the differences between and among women, including differences that are 'not strictly sexual' as well as those directly concerned with sexuality itself (de Lauretis 2000: 384). For her, lesbian sexuality is characterized by one woman's *conscious* desire for another, not woman-identification (de Lauretis 1994: 284).

In a film context, these issues came to a head in de Lauretis's dispute with another feminist critic Jackie Stacey, whose article 'Desperately

Seeking Difference' was published in *Screen* in 1987. In this article, Stacey looks at two films dealing with one woman's obsession with another: Susan Seidelman's *Desperately Seeking Susan* (1985) and Joseph Mankiewicz's *All About Eve* (1950). In *Desperately Seeking Susan*, for example, Roberta (Rosanna Arquette), a bored suburban housewife, pursues the carefree and streetwise Susan (played by Madonna). She follows Susan's lovelife through newspaper ads, wears a jacket that Susan has pawned, and carries her photo until amnesia finally leads her to become her role model. Stacey argues that, although neither *Desperately Seeking Susan* or *All About Eve* are lesbian films, they offer female spectators certain pleasures associated with women's active sexual desires – pleasures that 'cannot simply be reduced to a masculine heterosexual equivalent' (Stacey 2000: 456).

De Lauretis responded with a strong critique of Stacey's article. First of all, she maintains that these films are about identification, not desire. Both portray a younger and more 'childlike' woman seeking to be like, or to ascend to the position of, the other woman whether, as in *All About Eve*, 'to become a famous star like her, and to replace her as the object of desire of both her husband and the audience', or, as in *Desperately Seeking Susan*, 'to acquire her image as a woman liberated, free and "saturated with sexuality"' (de Lauretis 1994: 117). She points out that in psychoanalysis, 'this "childlike" wish is a kind of identification that is at once ego-directed, narcissistic, and *desexualized*' (de Lauretis 1994:117). She contrasts this, a form of ego-libido, with object-libido, which is sexual and involves desire (de Lauretis 1994: 118). It is the difference between wanting *to be* or *be like* the other woman (a form of identification) and wanting to *have* her (sexual desire). De Lauretis insists that the 'desire' between women is not sexual in these films – it is just a narcissistic fascination. Stacey has mistakenly equated the homosexual with the homosocial, 'i.e., woman-identified female bonding' (de Lauretis 1994: 120).

Stacey's argument, however, stems from a questioning of psycho-analytic film theory's 'rigid distinction between *either* desire *or* identification', which she believes 'fails to address the construction of desires which involve a specific interplay of both processes' (Stacey 2000: 464). Although Stacey does not consider it, the distinction between desire and identification is far from clear-cut in psychoanalytic litera-ture itself, as de Lauretis is well aware. Tactically, de Lauretis reasserts the orthodox distinction in this instance, but elsewhere much of her own work questions psychoanalytic ideas and radically reconfigures them. Nowhere is this more apparent than in her unorthodox reading of Freud's theory of fetishism, through which she unfolds her model of lesbian desire.

LESBIAN FETISHISM

It takes two women, not one, to make a lesbian.

(de Lauretis 1994: 92)

De Lauretis wants to articulate the specificity of lesbian sexuality, and sets herself the challenge of doing this within a psychoanalytic framework. If there could be a psychoanalytic theory of lesbian sexuality then this, she suggests in *The Practice of Love*, is what it would be. However, instead of revisiting the Oedipal scenario as Silverman and others have done, she offers a conception of 'limitless desire' beyond the mother, father and Oedipus, basing her theory of lesbian sexuality on her own self-analysis and analyses of lesbian fiction as well as on Freud's theory of fetishism. Despite his inability to understand female, let alone lesbian, sexuality, de Lauretis finds many parallels between Freud's endeavour and her own. Freud, too, founded many of his psychoanalytic theories on his self-analysis, also using literary examples, aware of their speculative, indeed subjective, nature. De Lauretis regards his theories as 'passionate fictions', based on his own gendered, racially-marked, socio-historical experiences. Nonetheless, 'for better or for worse', they are fictions that, she believes, resonate with her own experiences and those of other women of her culture and generation (de Lauretis 1994: xiv). She offers her own theory of lesbian sexuality as another subjective, 'passionate fiction' – yet one that, she hopes, will resonate with other lesbians.

There are, of course, obvious problems with using psychoanalysis for this purpose, and de Lauretis enumerates them thoroughly. Female homosexuality was largely ignored by psychoanalysis just as it had been by Victorian law. Moreover, the psychoanalytic accounts of lesbian sexuality that do exist are thought to be hopelessly wrong by many contemporary queer theorists, who almost unanimously reject psychoanalysis as a theoretical framework. However, within Freud's theories, de Lauretis uncovers a notion of the perverse nature of desire totally in keeping with queer theory's most radical insights.

In his 'Three Essays on the Theory of Sexuality', Freud queried the notion of 'normal' sexuality at a time when nineteenth-century sexologists like Krafft-Ebing and Havelock Ellis had laid the groundwork for both medical and popular views of homosexuality as a pathological condition. Unlike them, Freud speculates that the relationship between the sexual drive and its object is neither fixed nor innate: the sexual instinct is, initially, independent of its object; it is not rooted in nature or biology. Later, in 'Instincts and their Vicissitudes', he writes that the object of a drive is what is 'most variable' about it; it is 'not originally connected' with the drive, 'but becomes assigned to it only in consequence of being peculiarly fitted to make satisfaction possible' (Freud 1991c: 119).

In this view, 'perversions' like homosexuality are not a deviation from 'nature'. In fact, the drive itself works through detour and deviation, perpetually searching for objects peculiarly suited to meeting its aim of satisfaction. An interplay of different forces, between the external world and the psyche, between the social and the body, produces our desires, which are infinite in their possible permutations, dynamic and unpredictable, disputing the idea of a single 'normal' or 'natural' sexuality. Yet, at times Freud assumes that reproductive heterosexuality is the ideal and the norm, indeed the goal of human sexuality. But elsewhere this conventional, teleological view of sexuality is contradicted by his more radical insight that sexual 'norms' are enforced by cultural restrictions, which regulate the drives into socially permissible pleasures (de Lauretis 1994: 14). In this context, 'perverse' desire no longer means 'pathological' desire, for it is only 'deviant' with respect to social norms or conventions supporting particular structures of power, such as patriarchy.

In Freud's theory of fetishism, the fetish is used to deny the absence of a penis in women, specifically the mother. The process has the double character of disavowal – the fetishist at once knows that the mother does not have a penis but refuses to recognize that she hasn't. He invests his desire in another part of the body, hair, or clothing (e.g. women's undergarments), using that as a 'substitute' for the penis. This model of fetishism illustrates how desire operates through a constant process of substitution and displacement.

Freud claimed that there was no such thing as female fetishism; as women have no penis they have nothing to lose – they are 'already' castrated – so disavowal would not be an effective defensive measure for them. Following Mulvey, most feminist theorists have discussed women as objects of fetishism rather than its subjects or practitioners. But contrary to their thinking, ample evidence exists that women do fetishize and Freud himself once remarked that all women are clothes fetishists (cited in de Lauretis 1994: 273).

As a form of 'perverse' desire that subverts normative notions of sexuality, fetishism is invaluable to queer theory and politics. For, in fetishism, the sexual instinct has been diverted from its 'legitimate', reproductive object onto a non-reproductive one (de Lauretis 1994: 222). De Lauretis takes her cue from Leo Bersani and Ulysses Dutoit's 'queer' model of fetishism, derived from Freud but by reading against him. Here, unlike Freud's model, the phallus is not the privileged, original signifier of desire. In fact, desire is not fixed to a privileged object at all, but continually shifts to other objects and images. In Bersani and Dutoit's view, the fetish is not a phallic symbol, standing in for a real penis, but a 'fantasy-phallus', 'an inappropriate object precariously attached to a desiring-fantasy, unsupported by any perceptual memory', the original object of desire being lost to one's perception (cited in de Lauretis 1994: 225).

De Lauretis claims that Bersani and Dutoit's model of fetishism can apply to lesbian sexuality, where the lesbian knows that the woman she desires does not have a penis, nor would she want her to have one. Lesbian desire, too, involves a disavowal of castration but on very different terms from the classic male fetishist. De Lauretis contends that lesbian desire is founded upon a fantasy of castration, understood not as lack of a penis but as 'a narcissistic wound to the subject's body-image' (de Lauretis 1994: 262). In this model, a failure to validate the little girl's body-image occurs at the time of the castration complex, which establishes the paternal prohibition of access to the female body, not just the female body of the mother (taboo on incest) but also in oneself (taboo on masturbation) and in other women (taboo on perversion).

Unlike Freud's male fetishist, lesbian fetishism arises out of love of femininity rather than fear of it. In de Lauretis's theory, lesbian desire displaces the wish for that lost and denied libidinally-invested female body-image onto fetishes that both signify its loss and re-present it. The mechanism of disavowal holds at bay the threat of this loss: the lesbian thinks, 'I don't have it but I can/will have it', enabling her to seek satisfaction in another desirable female body-image (de Lauretis

1994: 262). The lesbian knows that nothing can fully replace her original lack but invests her desire in a fetish, 'a fantasy-phallus, an inappropriate object', which derives its erotic meaning from being placed within a personal fantasy scenario. For de Lauretis, 'the lesbian fetish is any object, any sign whatsoever that marks the difference and the desire between the lovers'; for example, it could be 'the erotic signal of her hair at the nape of her neck' (de Lauretis 1994: 228).

The lesbian fetish is a symbolic object laden with sociohistorical meanings from cultural and subcultural discourses (de Lauretis 1994: 228). Take, for example, the prolific use of masculine codes in lesbian representations and subcultures – the butch or 'mannish' lesbian, male drag, the use of dildos, all of which could be considered in terms of a masculinity fetish. The psychoanalytic notion of the lesbian masculinity complex would conceive of these 'in normatively hetero-sexual terms as the wish for a penis' (de Lauretis 1994: 276). De Lauretis, on the other hand, interprets them as an appropriation of the culturally available symbols that signify – both to the user and to others – an active sexual desire for women (de Lauretis 1994: 263).

De Lauretis invokes Foucault's notion of 'reverse discourse' to describe the way in which such lesbian self-representations come about. In *The History of Sexuality*, Foucault argues that the historical emer-gence of medical and legal discourses inquiring into areas of sexual 'perversity' created the possibility of a 'reverse discourse', allowing homosexuality 'to speak in its own behalf, to demand that its legiti-macy or "naturality" be acknowledged, often in the same vocabulary, using the same categories by which it was medically disqualified' (Foucault 1998: 101). The adoption of camp by gay men could be seen as a reverse discourse: in this view, gay men internalize the dominant discourse that constructs them as effeminate, and then translate that into their camp self-representation. Similarly, de Lauretis argues that the popularity of the lesbian masculinity fetish is due to its emergence within a cultural climate where dominant cultural discourses represent lesbianism as 'phallic pretension or male identification' (de Lauretis 1994: 308). These representations have been internalized by lesbians, reworked in their subjective fantasies, then have emerged again, in a re-signified form, in their self-representations – including speech, gesture, costume, body, and stance – as the butch or mannish lesbian.

Male drag has long been a lesbian trope and form of self-represen-tation, as one can see in Sarah Waters's intricately researched, popular lesbian novel *Tipping the Velvet* (1998) (also adapted for television), which is set in the Victorian era and populated by male impersonators at vaudeville theatres, high society mannish lesbians, and working-class Toms ('Tom' is Victorian slang for lesbian). Another reverse discourse that can signify the lesbian fetish is that of 'a quintessential, empowered, and exclusive or absolute femininity' (de Lauretis 1994: 264). This is a more recent development in lesbian subculture, once again re-signifying available dominant cultural representations (de Lauretis 1994: 102). In an exaggerated display of femininity, 'the femme performs the sexual power and seductiveness of the female body when offered to the butch for mutual narcissistic empowerment' (de Lauretis 1994: 264). In de Lauretis's account, the femme is not caught in the dilemma of accepting male-defined norms of femininity, any more than the butch can be seen to be usurping a 'masculine prerogative' (de Lauretis 1994: 108). For, in both instances, their masquerade is addressed to women, not to men.

De Lauretis comments that this fantasy of femininity, which is 'at once constrained and defiant', has found a new appeal in 'the popular imagination of all-female socio-sexual spaces, amazonic or matriarchal, ranging from girls' schools to prisons and from alternative worlds to convents and brothels' (de Lauretis 1994: 264–5). In such spaces, 'the female body is the site of a sexuality that is both incited and forbidden or regulated, but in either case female-directed and female-centred'. It is not hard to see why television series which are set in such spaces, such as *Prisoner: Cell Block H* (1979–86) or *Xena: Warrior Princess* (1995–2001), have attained lesbian cult status. De Lauretis adds: 'The elaborate scenarios of lesbian sadomasochism, too, hinge on the power and control of the sexual female body by and for women' (de Lauretis 1994: 265). What all these instances share is a fantasy scenario that sustains perverse desire through restaging and recovering a lost, fantasmatic female body, to which patriarchal culture has prohibited access.

SUMMARY

This chapter has shown how de Lauretis asserts the specificity of lesbian desire, first, through films that create the conditions of a different kind of visibility rather than reaffirming dominant representational codes, and then through her critique of feminist discourse, which conflates lesbian desire with woman identification. In contrast to standard feminist accounts of lesbian and female sexuality, which focus on the Oedipus Complex and the mother–daughter relationship, de Lauretis submits an account of lesbian desire that goes beyond the terms of the Oedipus Complex, exploring the mobility of fetishistic or perverse desire. Lesbian desire, she argues, is formed against the threat of castration, here conceived as a lack in the subject's body-ego, and compensated for by fetish objects that represent the lost and denied female body. De Lauretis's theory of lesbian sexuality is meant to be enabling, offering us a different way of conceiving how sexuality is 'implanted' in the subject. Her project fruitfully brings together Freud's psychosexual theories and Foucault's sociosexual theories, showing that these two thinkers' conceptions of sexuality are not as mutually exclusive as usually thought.

6

THE MONSTROUS-FEMININE

Horror has long been regarded as the least 'respectable' of film genres; it is, nevertheless, one of the most popular, making addictive viewing for its fans. Although psychoanalysis does not provide the only account of the horror film, with its concept of the unconscious it helps to unravel the genre's appeals to audiences' repressed fears and desires. This chapter focuses on Barbara Creed's psychoanalytic study of the horror film in her book *The Monstrous-Feminine*, first published in 1993. Here, Creed focuses on the horror film's figuration of woman-as-monster, drawing on Kristeva's notion of the abject, defined as that which 'disturbs identity, system, order' and 'does not respect borders, positions, rules' (Kristeva 1982: 4). The abject both fascinates and horrifies: it thrives on ambiguity and the transgression of taboos and boundaries. A defining theme throughout Creed's work, the notion of abject also appears in her later book *Media Matrix* (2003), where she extends it to the taste for the taboo and the sensational in television news, chat shows, reality television, the Internet, and women's romances. Creed's work as a whole attests to the continuing validity of psychoanalytic concepts for understanding not only horror films but also a broader popular culture.

Apart from studies such as Siegfried Kracauer's *From Caligari to Hitler* (1947), the horror genre received scant critical attention until the 1970s. Among the other early forays into the genre is Margaret

Tarratt's 'Monsters from the Id', first published in 1971, which applies a psychoanalytic reading to *The Thing* (1951) and *Forbidden Planet* (1956). However, it is the gay male critic Robin Wood's understanding of the horror film as a society's collective nightmare, staging the return of 'all that our civilization represses or oppresses', that is more widely acknowledged as defining psychoanalytic approaches to the genre (Wood 1986: 75). Wood first put forward his ideas in his 1978 essay, 'The Return of the Repressed', named after the Freudian idea that what is repressed into the unconscious always returns – re-surfacing in disguised or symbolic form. In the horror film, the return of the repressed is enacted in the form of the monster, who not only turns society's dominant norms upside down but also embodies what is repressed in us. The monster is our own and society's 'Other'.

While the monster changes its shape through history, attiring itself in the prevalent fears of the day, the categories it symbolizes as society's Other, according to Wood, include: women; the working class; other cultures; ethnic minorities; alternative political ideologies (for example, the threat of communism in 1950s stories about alien invaders); alternative sexualities (monsters are often identified with homosexuality or bisexuality, especially in vampire films); and children (films like *The Exorcist* [1973] or *The Omen* [1976] figure the child-as-monster). Our attitude to the monster is frequently ambivalent: although society teaches us to be morally appalled by its terrible deeds, rarely is the monster presented as wholly unsympathetic. Indeed, part of us takes delight in its actions and identifies with them.

The monster's Otherness is often configured as a bodily difference. Most horror films give special emphasis to a monster's gender, indicating that sexual difference and gender are among the genre's key concerns. Think of titles such as *Attack of the 50-Foot Woman* (1958), with its publicity poster (reproduced in Creed's *The Monstrous-Feminine*) depicting woman as a 'destructive colossus' wreaking havoc on the streets (Creed 2001). In the rest of this chapter we will see how Creed adapts Wood's perspective and that of other feminist or psychoanalytic critics to present her own powerful contribution to cultural analysis.

THE ABJECT

In *The Monstrous-Feminine*, Creed extends to the horror film the structures of abjection that Kristeva, in her book *Powers of Horror* (first published in 1980), discusses in relation to literature. Although the abject is, ultimately, part of ourselves, we reject it, expelling it and locating it outside the self, designating it as 'not-me', in order to protect our boundaries. In her first category of abjection, Creed includes bodily wastes such as 'shit, blood, urine, and pus', as well as dead bodies, which are 'the ultimate in abjection' (Creed 2001: 9). For example, the living dead (zombies, vampires) and other bodies without souls (ghouls, robots, androids) populate horror films, which abound in images of corpses and bodily wastes (blood, vomit, saliva). Another instance drawn from Kristeva is food loathing, as induced by (for example) the skin on the top of hot milk, which many people find disgusting. Food loathing, Creed notes, is a frequent locus of abjection in the horror film, especially those involving flesh-eating zombies.

The second aspect of abjection in the horror film lies in the collapsing of boundaries or boundary ambiguities. The monster is what 'crosses or threatens to cross the "border"', for example, the border between human and non-human; natural and supernatural; normal and abnormal gender behaviour and sexual desire; the clean, proper, well-formed, and the dirty or deformed body (Creed 2001: 11). Finally, Creed's third class of the abject is the maternal. Female monstrosity in the horror film is nearly always depicted in relation to mothering and reproductive functions. According to Kristeva, the female body, especially the mother's body, is aligned with the abject because it does not hide its debt to nature. But, as Creed emphasizes – more than Kristeva does – 'woman is not, by her very nature, an abject being'; rather, patriarchal ideology constructs her as such (Creed 2001: 83).

Kristeva argues that an infant makes its mother's body abject in its struggle to become a separate being, to free itself from the *chora* or maternal receptacle (see Chapter 3 for Silverman's discussion of this topic). As well as through the taboo of incest, separation from the mother is enforced by ideas that her body is polluted, due to its association with menstruation, childbirth, and the infant's toilet training. It is the mother who first teaches the child about the clean and unclean parts of the body – Kristeva uses the label of the 'semiotic' to describe this 'primal mapping of the body'(Kristeva 1982: 72). This 'maternal authority', characterized by a guilt-free attitude to the body and its wastes, is later repressed when the child enters the Symbolic Order – the realm of language and social codes, which is associated with the Law of the Father and marked by prohibition. In the Symbolic Order, bodily wastes are regarded as filthy and shameful.

Historically, the function of purifying the abject, forming and safe-guarding boundaries and defining what it means to be human and civilized, was performed by religious ritual. That function has now devolved, Kristeva asserts, to art (Kristeva 1982: 17). In Creed's view, the art form that best befits this role is the horror film: its 'central ideological project' is to bring about a confrontation with the abject in order, finally, to expel it, and permit boundaries between the civilized and uncivilized, human and non-human, to be redrawn (2001: 14).

The abject terrifies us but fascinates us all the same. Horror films attest to the audience's desire to confront 'sickening, horrific images', to witness the taboo, which is what provokes shock and terror; then, once we have taken our fill, 'to throw up, throw out, eject the abject' (Creed 2001: 10). When people say 'that film made me sick' they touch on this function of abjection in a literal sense. The depiction of the abject allows the spectator to indulge vicariously in taboo forms of behaviour from the safety of his or her seat, before order is finally restored: this is the horror film's central appeal.

Furthermore, because the maternal body plays a key role in the construction of the abject, it has become the underlying image of all that is monstrous in the horror film, signifying that which threatens the stability of the Symbolic Order. For the spectator, situated within the Symbolic, the images portrayed by horror films inspire loathing and disgust, yet they also hark back to a time when bodily products were not regarded with embarrassment and shame, when the mother–child relationship was characterized by 'an untrammelled pleasure in "playing" with the body and its wastes' (Creed 2001: 13). Many films represent the fear of being reabsorbed into the mother's body. For example, *Psycho* features a tenacious mother who refuses to give up her child, preventing it from taking up its position in the Symbolic. *The Exorcist*, on the other hand, dramatizes a battle between 'fathers' and 'mothers': between the priestly Fathers (Karras and Merrin), who represent paternal Symbolic law, and the demon-possessed adolescent girl Regan, who lives with her single parent mother. Regan graphically displays and wallows in bodily wastes, evoking the abject and the repressed world of maternal authority: she urinates on the carpet, spits green bile, and masturbates with a crucifix until blood spurts from her vagina. Through horror films such as these, the repressed semiotic *chora* disrupts the rational order of the paternal symbolic and challenges the human subject's apparent stability (Creed 2001: 38).

THE ARCHAIC MOTHER

Female monsters abound in mythology: the snake-locked Gorgon Medusa, the deadly Sirens, and the bloodthirsty Hindu goddess Kali are just some of the examples mentioned by Creed. For her, many of the female monsters in the horror film appear to have evolved from these kinds of mythical archetypes. Yet women in the horror film are typically seen as victims, rather than monsters – terrified and preyed upon like Fay Wray by King Kong. Some horror film critics have even claimed that there are no 'great' female monsters comparable to the male tradition presided over by Frankenstein and Dracula. When female monstrosity *is* discussed, Creed claims, it is nearly always in terms of the Freudian idea of woman as man's castrated other.

Creed does not dispute that many films do explore the idea of the castrated woman, but she argues that the central figure of female monstrosity in the horror genre is not the castrated woman, but her 'alter ego', the castrating woman. The reason why critics have avoided looking at the construction of woman as castrator is that here it is more obvious that the woman is not herself castrated; rather, it is the male, who is threatened with castration. The castrating woman is not passive like the castrated woman. She represents an active monster. Although this by itself does not make her a 'feminist' or 'liberated' figure, the revelation of woman as castrator does challenge patriarchal views that woman is essentially a victim.

Creed's project is to uncover the many *different* aspects of woman-as-monster: the archaic mother, the monstrous womb, vampire, witch, possessed body, castrating mother, and deadly *femme castratrice*. What Creed calls 'the archaic mother' differs from Kristeva's conception of the mother in *Powers of Horror*. Kristeva's mother of the semiotic *chora* is a pre-Oedipal mother, whose existence is defined in relation to the family and the Symbolic Order. The archaic mother, on the other hand, is another aspect of the maternal figure, whose existence has been repressed in patriarchal ideology. She is the primeval mother of every-thing – a parthenogenetic mother, creating all by herself, without the need for a father; she is a pre-phallic mother, existing prior to know-ledge of the phallus. ('Parthenogenetic' – deriving from the Greek, meaning 'virgin birth' – refers to the common mythological trope of procreating by oneself; other examples include Zeus, who gave birth to the goddess Athena from his ear, and the Virgin Mary's 'immaculate conception'.)

In her mythological incarnations, the archaic mother is known as Nu Kwa (in China), Coatlicue (in Mexico), Gaia (in Greece), and Nammu (in Sumer) (Creed 2001: 24). She exists outside morality: as the giver of life she can, equally, take it away. Creed contends that, in *Alien* (1979), the figure of the mother appears in the guise of the archaic mother. As the creature who lays the eggs, she never materializes in person (although she does in the sequels), but her image underlies the film's images of birth, its representations of the 'primal scene', the uterine imagery of winding corridors leading towards internal chambers, the voice of the ship's life-support system (actually called 'Mother'), and the shape-shifting alien itself.

The 'primal scene' is about origins; it is the child's fantasy about 'where babies come from'. Children often conceive the primal scene as a monstrous act, imagining animals or mythical creatures as participants. Creed suggests that mythological stories where gods take the

PRIMAL FANTASIES

Creed makes use of the notion of primal or 'original' fantasies developed by Jean Laplanche and J.-B. Pontalis in their paper 'Fantasy and the Origins of Sexuality', first published in 1964. Through a close re-reading of Freud, they assert that primal fantasies 'provide a representation of, and a solution to, the major enigmas which confront the child' (Laplanche and Pontalis 1968: 11). Children use them to fill in the gaps in their understanding of adult sexuality. They include primal scene fantasies (about where babies come from), seduction fantasies (about the origins of sexuality), and castration fantasies (about the origin of sexual difference). Creed believes these are all fantasies upon which the horror film draws.

Elizabeth Cowie's article 'Fantasia' (1984), which links the private fantasies discussed in psychoanalysis to the public fantasies of cinema, is another influence. Cowie uses Laplanche and Pontalis's notion of fantasy as the setting or *mise-en-scène* of desire', where the subject 'appears caught up himself in the sequence of images' (Cowie 1984: 87; Laplanche and Pontalis 1968: 17). She argues that, although the terms of sexual difference in a film may be fixed – for example, 'active or passive, feminine or masculine, mother or son, father or daughter' – a number of different positions are open to the spectator, whose viewpoint and identifications are fluid and mobile (Cowie 1984: 87).

form of animals and copulate with humans, such as 'Leda and the Swan', could be seen as renderings of the primal scene (Creed 2001: 18). Horror films also rework the primal scene, exploring alternative means of reproduction in their fantasy scenarios. For example, in *The Brood* (1979), the mother-figure Nola Carveth gives birth to her horrific offspring through her armpits, while the horror science-fiction *Invasion of the Body Snatchers* (1956) presents aliens reproducing asexually as vegetal pods.

Alien features a number of birthing scenes. In the opening, the camera tracks along the corridors of the ship *Nostromo*, into a womb-like chamber where 'Mother' awakes the crew from their cryogenic pods. She is a parthenogenetic mother, as she is their 'sole parent and sole life-support' (Creed 2001: 18). Although the birthing appears clean and painless, devoid of blood or trauma, this mother is also bloody and amoral, both giver and taker of life, having been programmed by the Company to procure the alien, 'all other priorities rescinded', including her crew's lives. In the film's next representation of the primal scene, Kane, Lambert, and Dallas visit a derelict spaceship where the alien is discovered. The ship's entrance is a 'vaginal' opening, its sides curved like a pair of outspread legs. Unlike the *Nostromo*, its cavernous interior is moist and dark. Kane descends a shaft into another womb-like chamber filled with eggs. When he attempts to touch one, the egg opens, releasing the creature inside, which thrusts its tail down his throat to inseminate him, smothering him. Later, Kane dies, giving birth to his monstrous offspring through his stomach. For Creed, this scene enacts 'an extreme primal scene phantasy where the subject imagines travelling back inside the womb to watch his/her parents having sexual intercourse, perhaps to watch themselves being conceived' (Creed 2001: 19). The alien's birth from Kane's stomach also evokes familiar childhood misconceptions about reproduction – that babies are conceived orally (for example, by the mother eating a special food) and that they grow in tummies.

At this point, Creed draws on Roger Dadoun's analysis of the archaic mother in the Dracula variant of the vampire film. For Dadoun, the small enclosed village, the pathway leading through the forest to the central enclosure of the castle, its winding stairways, cobwebs, dark vaults, and damp earth are 'elements which all relate back to the *imago* of the bad archaic mother' (Dadoun 1989: 53) He suggests Dracula, who emerges in the midst of this, with a piercing gaze, pointed teeth, and rigid stature, is a form of fetish, a 'substitute for the mother's penis' (Dadoun 1989: 55). According to this interpretation, the monster is an intermediary for the archaic mother and represents her missing phallus – even though, Creed remarks, the archaic mother does not need the phallus; 'she is all-powerful and absolute unto herself' (Creed 2001: 21). In her analysis, the archaic mother is attributed a phallus by a patriarchal ideology unable to conceive of female desire other than in its own terms. This explains why filmic manifestations of the archaic mother are nearly always nightmare images, associated with abjection, darkness, dispossession, and death: the archaic mother is not an inherently negative image, but patriarchal discourses reconstruct her as such. However, in films where the main vampire is female, such as *The Hunger* (1983), the archaic mother's 'shadowy presence' does not need to be inferred through the medium of the male vampire, for there 'the vampire *is* the archaic mother' (Creed 2001: 72).

Comparisons can be drawn between *Alien* and the Dracula film: the alien originates in the archaic mother's womb, yet has phallic traits, such as the tail, which Kane's face-hugger inserts into his mouth or the undeniably penile chest-burster. Creed suggests that the archaic mother's phallus works fetishistically, but differently from the Freudian sense: her fetish-phallus does not cover over her so-called castration or lack; rather, it covers over and disavows her imaginary castrating *vagina dentata*. Literally meaning 'toothed vagina', the *vagina dentata* is a motif that can be traced not only in Western culture – Creed cites the Greek mythological figure Scylla, a beautiful woman in her upper body whose nether regions 'consist of three snapping hellhounds' – but in folklore and myth throughout the world (Creed 2001: 106). She comments: 'Despite local variations, the myth generally states that women are terrifying because they have teeth in their vaginas and that the women must be tamed or the teeth somehow removed or softened – usually by a hero figure – before intercourse can safely take place' (Creed 2001: 2). To give a filmic example, in *Basic Instinct* (1992) Michael Douglas plays Nick Curran, a detective hunting for a female killer whose weapon is an ice pick. He becomes sexually involved with his prime suspect, Catherine Tramell (Sharon Stone), who is found not guilty. In the final scene, as Nick and Catherine once again have sex, an ice pick is revealed under the bed, Catherine's symbolic *vagina dentata*. As Creed remarks, *Basic Instinct* intimates that 'having sex with women is an extremely dangerous business' (Creed 2001: 124).

The prevalence of this myth is clear evidence that woman is feared as a castrator. The motif of *vagina dentata*, Creed states, portrays 'the female genitals as a trap, a black hole which threatens to swallow [men] up and cut them to pieces' (2001: 106). Examples can be found in surrealist art: Salvador Dali's take on the *vagina dentata* is illustrated in *The Monstrous-Feminine* (Plate 14), with a naked woman posing with a lobster placed over her vagina. The mythical *vagina dentata* links the threat of castration to the threat of being devoured. In the Dracula film, we see it in the vampire's fanged mouth. In *Jaws* (1975), it appears as the shark's voracious, bloody maw. In *Alien*, it turns up in the monster's double set of snapping jaws and saliva-dripping razor-teeth.

MEDUSA'S HEAD

The Greek mythological gorgon Medusa is renowned for her terrible glance, which turned men to stone. Many vampire films testify to her legacy of fear, showing the female vampire's deadly nature by associating her with Medusa (Creed 2001: 60). According to Freud, Medusa's decapitated head represents 'woman as a being who frightens and repels because she is castrated' (Freud 1955: 274). He overlooks the fact that 'with her head of writhing snakes, huge mouth, lolling tongue and boar's tusks, the Medusa is also regarded by historians of myth as a particularly nasty version of the *vagina dentata*' (Creed 2001: 111). According to Creed, Medusa horrifies not because she passively resembles the castrated female genitals but because she actively threatens to castrate. Freud interprets the numerous snakes upon her head as phallic fetish objects that, although frightening in themselves, serve to alleviate the horror of the absent penis. This, Creed points out, is yet another oversight. After all, snakes have capacious mouths and pointed fangs: 'The Medusa's entire visage is alive with images of toothed vaginas, poised and waiting to strike. No wonder her male victims were rooted to the spot with fear' (Creed 2001: 111).

Creed finds other instances where Freud has wilfully repressed the power of the castrating woman in his case history of 'Little Hans'. Hans suffered from an anxiety and phobia about horses. Freud interpreted this in terms of his theory of the Oedipus Complex, where the father is feared as castrator and the mother is believed to be castrated. However, Creed argues that the real source of Hans's fear is not his father but his mother, for it is she who utters the threat of castration, as a punishment for masturbation. Creed casts doubt on Freud's assumption that all children initially think the mother has a penis like the father and then later realize she is different and therefore castrated (Creed 2001: 93). According to her, Hans knows that his mother's genitals are different from his own and fears them not as castrated but as castrating. That man constructs woman as castrator and displaces his fear onto her is something Freud does not consider:

> Perhaps one should conclude that acceptance of the notion of 'woman the castrator' rather than 'woman the castrated' is not only threatening to Freud as a man but also damaging to his theories of penis envy in women, the castration crisis and the role he assigns the father in the transmission of culture.
>
> (Creed 2001: 121)

Creed, on the other hand, emphasizes the mother's crucial and active role in the child's entry into the Symbolic Order and suggests fear of the castrating mother may be decisive in bringing about the rupture between herself and her child; this dimension of the mother is ignored in film criticism, just as it is in psychoanalytic theory. Challenging Freud and Lacan, she insists that the mother *can* be identified with the Law, and that the Symbolic is not necessarily patriarchal; it is patriarchal ideology's signifying practices that construct the maternal body as abject and non-symbolic. In this, Creed goes beyond her main influence, Kristeva, who does not question the patriarchal character of the Symbolic.

THE DEADLY *FEMME CASTRATRICE*

Male castration anxiety has created two particular representations of the monstrous-feminine in the horror film: (1) woman as castrator, and (2) the castrated woman. The slasher film, with *Psycho* as its prototype, portrays women in both roles: in *Psycho*, the younger woman, Marion, represents the castrated woman – slashed by the killer behind the shower curtain, her body physically cut up to resemble a bleeding wound – but the real source of horror is the castrating mother, whose personality has overtaken her son's.

In her essay, 'Her Body, Himself: Gender in the Slasher Film', originally published in 1987, Carol Clover defines the slasher film by its use of knives or other sharp weapons, rather than guns (Clover 1996: 79). According to her, its other staple generic features are: the killer, often a psychopath; the 'terrible place', usually a house or tunnel where the victims find themselves trapped; and the 'Final Girl', who survives and subdues or kills the killer after he has murdered her friends one by one. For Creed, the heroine of the slasher film is a castrator but Clover, who submits to Freudian logic in this respect, does not categorize her as such; instead she says the Final Girl is phallicized, given masculine traits and a boyish name – for example, Laurie (Jamie Lee Curtis) in *Halloween* (1978) while, in *Alien*, the heroine's androgynous name Ripley (Sigourney Weaver) indicates the film's debt to the slasher tradition. Clover describes the Final Girl as 'a figurative male', who allows the mostly male audience of the genre to identify across the lines of gender (Clover 1996: 100). In Clover's view, the Final Girl has 'the "active investigating gaze" normally reserved for males' (Clover 1996: 93). She also looks *at* the killer, brandishing a sharp weapon such as a knife, sledgehammer, chainsaw, or knitting needle, in order to combat him on his own terms. On the basis of all these 'phallic symbols', Clover refers to the 'shared masculinity' of the killer and the Final Girl, and also their 'shared femininity', for the killer suffers castration at her hands (Clover 1996: 94).

Disagreeing with this, Creed argues that just 'because the heroine is represented as resourceful, intelligent, and dangerous, it does not follow that she should be seen as a pseudo man' (Creed 2001: 127). She cites a number of non-boyishly named slasher film heroines, such as Alice in *Friday the 13th* (1980) and Nancy in *A Nightmare on Elm Street* (1984). To this list, one could add the sword-wielding Beatrice (Uma Thurman) in *Kill Bill* (2003). Creed avers that 'the avenging heroine of the slasher film is not the Freudian phallic woman whose image is designed to allay castration anxiety . . . but the deadly *femme castratrice*' (Creed 2001: 127).

The *femme castratrice* is an all-powerful, all-destructive figure, who 'arouses a fear of castration and death while simultaneously playing on a masochistic desire for death, pleasure and oblivion [in men]' (Creed 2001: 130). The heroines of rape-revenge and slasher films belong in this category, as does the dangerous heroine of *Basic Instinct*, through whom the detective cultivates a masochistic desire for death. In films featuring the *femme castratrice*, it is the male body, not the female body, that bears the burden of castration. The spectator is invited to identify with the avenging female castrator – 'the *femme castratrice* controls the sadistic gaze; the male victim is her object' (Creed 2001: 153).

Thus, the presence of woman as an active monster throws into question theories of spectatorship derived from Mulvey, which align the male character or spectator with the active, controlling gaze and place the woman as the object of that gaze. This model cannot explain the structure of looks produced in the horror film. Although many of the anxieties she analyzes are male, Creed speculates that the horror genre holds particular appeals for the female spectator, who perhaps feels 'empowered' by identifying with the female castrator (Creed 2001: 155). However, having made this rather bold point, Creed just states that spectators frequently switch their allegiances between monster and victim, depending on their wishes at the time (to terrify or be terrified) and the filmic codes that encourage varying degrees of identification with either figure.

So, not all pleasures or terrors offered by the horror genre are male-defined. Creed refutes the argument that only male spectators enjoy identifying with aggressive or violent heroines, for this assumes 'that only phallic masculinity is violent and that femininity is never violent – not even in the imagination' (Creed 2001: 155). Moreover, the idea that women are non-violent and peaceful has long been used by patriarchal ideology to control women. But, although female directors have ventured into the horror/slasher genres – Amy Jones's *Slumber Party Massacre* (1982), Kathryn Bigelow's *Near Dark* (1987), and Jane Campion's *In the Cut* (2003) – together with action, horror is one of the popular genres that female directors are least likely to direct. Creed, however, maintains:

> The reason women do not make horror films is not that the 'female' unconscious is fearless, without its monsters, but because women still lack access to the means of production in a system that continues to be male-dominated in all areas.
>
> (Creed 2001: 156).

CRISIS TV

In *Media Matrix*, Creed turns her attention to more culturally specific forms of viewing horror. Since it is constructed by whatever crosses the boundaries between civilized and uncivilized, conceptions of the abject differ from society to society. Creed contends that 'in the West, where people enjoy relatively comfortable modes of living, the public has turned more and more to the media as the main avenue for contact with, and understanding of, the abject' (Creed 2003: 9). The media (including newspapers, television dramas, and documentaries) cover sensational events, extreme forms of human behaviour, and world crises, frequently delving into taboo areas. Media images of war, violence, torture, death, disaster, and deviant sexual behaviour deliver abjection to the public daily. Popular media from television chat shows and Internet chat rooms to pornography, comics, and women's romances create forums where boundaries are crossed and standard, acceptable forms of behaviour and moral values are breached. Confessional television and chat shows, for example, thrive on the exposure of aberrant details in their participants' lives.

Not only have the media taken over the role of religion in drawing the lines between the acceptable and the taboo, they have also, Creed suggests, adopted the responsibility of a ritual guide in a progressively secular world, steering the public on a journey into 'unknown spaces', then returning us to 'familiar ground' (Creed 2003: 10). Just consider the format of television news. Although occasionally interspersed by uplifting stories (for example, the heroism of rescuers in a tragedy), the news mostly focuses on the horrific and abject (such as the hunt for bodies of missing persons, or images of the injured victims of war or disaster). It often concludes with a light-hearted item ('And finally . . .'), which reassuringly redraws the boundaries and returns us to familiar everyday norms.

Creed gives particular attention to a phenomenon she calls 'crisis TV'. The term refers to news reports of disasters – war, terrorism, genocide, torture, fire, flood, tornado – that endanger human life, causing people to die, usually in a 'painful and horrific manner' (Creed 2003: 177). Crisis TV, too, makes us confront the abject or the limits of 'the possible, the tolerable, the thinkable' but, unlike reality television for example, it is not intended to entertain (Creed 2003: 171).

Reporting 'live' from location, and using the formats of new digital media, the Internet and computer simulations, crisis TV creates the impression of immediacy and transparency. While many other interpretations, especially of the events of 9/11, have emphasized their spectacular real-time mediatization (see Baudrillard 2002), Creed alerts us to the fact that crisis TV is heavily constructed and interventionist. It always attempts to contain or censor the transmitted material in order to avoid upsetting the viewer. 'In crisis TV, the scenes of disaster appear transparent, seeming to unfold as they happen – in reality, the coverage has been carefully edited. . . . If one compares newspaper reports of the devastation at the World Trade Centre with television images, it is evident that most of the truly horrific sights were not displayed', including the hundreds of mutilated corpses strewn around the streets (Creed 2003: 179). The television coverage studiously avoided those sorts of images; it also limited the number of eyewitness accounts disclosing harrowing details for which the audience was simply not prepared. While reality television strives to capture everything, including extremities of human behaviour, crisis TV attempts to televise real crises but deletes what is most shocking. News presenters frequently issue warnings if forthcoming images are likely to disturb some of their viewers. Through the presenter, 'crisis TV performs the role of a liminal guide, one that accompanies the viewer into an underworld of horror and pain but ensures that journey is not too unbearable to watch' (Creed 2003: 182).

SUMMARY

This chapter has explored Creed's theory that horror films bring about a confrontation with the abject, defined as that which transgresses civilized boundaries. In an increasingly secular world, horror films serve the function of a purification rite, enabling audiences to encounter those things that threaten definitions of the human and the civilized, then to expel them and reassert normal boundaries. The notion of woman-as-monster or 'monstrous-feminine' in the horror film is often tied to the reproductive functions of the female body, which is constructed as abject in patriarchal cultures. The presence of active female monsters in horror films nonetheless challenges patriarchal views that women are basically passive victims. Drawing attention to fears of woman as castrator, Creed contests Freud's idea that woman only horrifies because she is assumed to be castrated. She also interrogates the notion that the father is the sole representative of the Law and the Symbolic Order, suggesting that fears of the castrating mother play a crucial cultural role. The role of woman as active monster, moreover, calls into question the theory of the male gaze and generates forms of identification for the female spectator. In her later work, Creed explores contemporary media such as the Internet and news reportage of disasters – 'crisis TV' has given birth to new ways of viewing horror and confronting the abject.

7

MASCULINITY
IN CRISIS

With the advances of the feminist and gay liberation movements and the need for differently-skilled workers in the post-industrial work-place, men are nowadays being forced to behave differently *as* men. Western media often present (white) heterosexual men as 'victims' of these changes, with women and gays making social and psychological gains at their expense. The concept of 'masculinity in crisis' has entered the popular arena, with bestsellers like Robert Bly's *Iron John* (1990) and films like *Fight Club* (1999) debating how men can 'reclaim' their masculinity, harking back nostalgically to an era when men were 'real' men. However, in feminist film theory, the concept of 'masculinity in crisis' refers not so much to 'a contemporary "crisis" of manhood', where the meaning of 'being a man' is assumed to be something stable and which has now been lost, but to the notion of masculinity itself as 'theoretically and historically *troubled*' (Penley and Willis 1988: 4).

Critical interest in the topic of masculinity is a direct outcome of the feminist movement's insight that gender is socially constructed, rather than a natural category. However, the term 'man' has long been equated with humanity in general, taken to be unmarked and universal. Partly due to this, it has been less apparent to critics – at least until the 1980s – that masculinity, like femininity, is also 'an effect of culture – a construction, a performance, a masquerade – rather than a universal and unchanging essence' (Cohan and Hark 1996: 7). The study of masculinity reveals that 'men' and 'male subjectivity' are historically mutable and ideologically unstable, constantly constructed and reconstructed in representation – including films and other popular media.

Feminist film theorists have, therefore, begun to interrogate the monolithic conception of 'Man' implied within their own theoretical framework: for example, the masculinized spectator that narrative cinema is said to have addressed and the fantasies of voyeurism and fetishism that were thought to encompass the pleasures of male spectatorship. In a move towards discussing masculinity in more specific ways, they have acknowledged the existence of multiple masculinities; each diversely affected by positions of class, race, sexuality, age; each with a different relationship to the institutions and discourses of power (Penley and Willis 1988: 4). With this broader insight into masculinity, it is no longer tenable to align men on one side of the power line and women on the other. This is what Kaja Silverman suggests in her investigation into masculinity, which is the focus of this chapter.

The binary oppositions that Mulvey deployed in 'Visual Pleasure and Narrative Cinema' equate masculinity with activity, sadism, and voyeurism and femininity with passivity, masochism, and exhibitionism. Since her early work, Silverman has questioned the truthfulness of these cultural binaries, including the underlying assumption that male pleasure always revolves around mastery (Silverman 1980: 2). Her writings on masculinity constitute some of the most nuanced feminist interventions in this area. In her article, 'Masochism and Subjectivity' (1980), she reveals male masochism and lack as a 'cultural secret', which has been preserved by the equation of the male with active, sadistic, voyeuristic tendencies and the female with tendencies to be passive, masochistic, and 'to-be-looked-at' (Silverman 1980: 8). In her book *Male Subjectivity at the Margins* (1992), which revisits a number of issues that she tackled in earlier books and articles, she explores masculinities which are socially constructed as being 'marginal' to the norms of 'classic' or 'conventional' masculinity. These masochistic, non-phallic, and wounded masculinities highlight the lack at the heart of male subjectivity. In so doing, they expose the fictive character of normative or 'phallic' masculinity which, according to Silverman, is today founded upon a denial of lack, passivity, masochism, and specularity or susceptibility to the gaze.

THE DOMINANT FICTION

As already indicated in Chapter 3, Silverman's work engages critically with Lacanian psychoanalysis. Despite insisting that the penis is not the phallus, Lacan often makes the phallus into a universal signifier of desire. Silverman, on the other hand, reads the phallus as a culturally variable symbol of lack. According to Lacan, access to language and entry into the Symbolic Order installs lack into the human subject, but Silverman believes that lack has 'a range of possible representatives' and that the link between the phallus and Symbolic Law is ideological, rather than inevitable (Silverman 1992: 38). This lack or 'symbolic castration' is universal for both men and women; it is the unavoidable condition of all subjectivity: we forgo any possibility of wholeness when we become subordinated to a discursive order that precedes us and speaks for us. Due to universal castration, no one can possess the phallus, which symbolizes an unattainable wholeness. However, in what Silverman calls 'the dominant fiction' – the images and stories through which a society configures consensus, images which films draw upon and help to shape – there is an imaginary equation between the penis and the phallus, which cements the male subject's identification with power and privilege.

Classic male subjectivity is ideologically constructed through this *misrecognition* of the penis as the phallus; this is what enables it to deny its own castration. The term misrecognition here has all the connotations of imaginary distortion that it has in Althusser's theory of ideology as well as in Lacan's theories. Silverman agrees with Althusser that, in ideology, our relationship to reality is imbued with the imaginary: society's consensus about what is 'real' is not merely a matter of 'rational agreement' but of 'imaginary affirmation' – a form of recognition that is also a *mis*recognition (Silverman 1992: 24). The idea of this ideologically-distorted reality is epitomized by her use of the term 'dominant fiction', which she borrows from another ideology analyst, Jacques Rancière (Silverman 1992: 30).

The dominant fiction 'forms the stable core around which a nation's and a period's "reality" coheres' (Silverman 1992: 41–2). Its most important image of unity is the family, which forms the traditional model for the construction of all other collective identities (community, town, nation). Above all, however, the dominant fiction's most privileged term is the phallus. Silverman writes: 'If ideology is central

MISRECOGNITION

Silverman adopts this term from the works of Althusser and Lacan. Althusser uses it to describe the way in which ideology commands belief. A person on the street who instantly turns around upon hearing the police call, 'Hey you there!' (mis)recognizes that the hail is 'really' addressed to him and is thereby 'sutured' into ideology. In Lacan's writings, misrecognition (in French, *méconnaissance*) is the basis of the ego, formed during the Mirror Stage, where the child identifies with an image outside itself, usually its reflection in the mirror. Like the subject sutured into ideology, the child has the sensation of 'Yes, it really is me!' (Silverman 1992: 20). That recognition of its image is a *mis*recognition because the image is whole and coherent, unlike the child who experiences itself as fragmented. To describe the infant's jubilant identification with its mirror image, Lacan uses the term 'captation', evoking the infant's 'capture' and 'captivation' by the imaginary. Captation also occurs when the subject identifies with other external images – including cultural representations. There, too, it (mis)recognizes itself. The Mirror Stage thus forms part of the series of misrecognitions through which the ego is constituted. It signals that the ego, which we think of as the core of identity or bearer of reality, is actually illusory.

to the maintenance of classic masculinity, the affirmation of classic masculinity is equally central to the maintenance of our governing "reality"' (Silverman 1992: 16). In other words, the collective belief of our society is so invested in the equation between the penis and phallus, upon which it depends for its 'reality', that a disconnection of those two terms can lead to loss of belief in the dominant fiction as a whole – i.e. a loss of belief in what passes for 'reality' in that society. In Silverman's account, therefore, any crisis in masculinity has enormous political implications: it is a key site within which to renegotiate our relationship with ideology.

The dominant fiction brings individuals into line with a given Symbolic Order by encouraging normative desires and identifications. The main vehicle of 'our' current dominant fiction is the positive Oedipus Complex, which accommodates us to the Name-of-the-Father, soliciting our belief in the (paternal) family and the sufficiency of the male subject. It upholds the equivalence between the penis and the phallus, but also between the actual father, who is by nature inadequate and flawed, and the Symbolic Father, imagined to be god-like and omnipotent. Although the family and the phallus are core elements of our dominant fiction, they co-exist intimately with other, secondary elements, arising from class, race, ethnicity, religion, gender, and national ideologies. Some secondary elements have helped to define the dominant fiction's main terms; for example, think of Christianity's conception of God, the heavenly Father.

'A loss of belief in secondary elements can precipitate a crisis in the primary ones', Silverman writes, but 'withdrawal of belief from the core components will always jeopardize . . . the coherence of the larger social formation' (Silverman 1992: 48). Silverman does not merely diagnose our ideological reality but theorizes how it may be changed, at both the psychic and cultural levels; indeed these two levels are always intertwined. What occurs within the psyche is cultural, while cultural forces work only by engaging psyches, through mechanisms such as fantasy, imaginary captation, and the positive Oedipus Complex. But Silverman is also careful to suggest that the psyche can go beyond the limits of that Complex; its desires and identifications can evade and reject the dominant fiction. Moreover, the dominant fiction itself is variable and can be changed. Discursive practices can challenge and transform it and the feminist and gay movements have already contested it.

The fact that the public majority sees the ideologies of these radical movements as threatening – as upsetting the very foundations of their 'world' and destroying everything they believe to be 'true' – testifies to their reluctance to relinquish belief in the dominant fiction. Numerous forces work to keep the dominant fiction in place. Silverman suggests there is 'a whole host of competing ideologies' struggling for access to the dominant fiction's 'belief effect' and thus always harnessing themselves to its core elements (Silverman 1992: 49). In today's society, capitalism is one such competing ideology; and, in the past, there have been others, including fascism in 1930s Germany, where the *Führer* acted as the nation's Symbolic Father.

What makes Silverman's analysis of the ideology of masculinity an important feminist project is that it stresses the implications for the female subject throughout. As in *The Acoustic Mirror* (see Chapter 3), so in *Male Subjectivity at the Margins*, she argues that the typical male subject deposits his castration or lack at the site of female subjectivity, while refusing to recognize his own 'lack'. Through mechanisms of projection, disavowal, and fetishism, the conventional male subject denies not only castration but also specularity and alterity (the experience of otherness). In Silverman's Lacanian framework, these are the inescapable conditions of all subjectivity but they are usually only consciously experienced by females. Indeed, the category of 'femininity' can be seen as a product of the denial of such conditions on the part of the male.

However, in the films that Silverman analyzes, it is not just men who fetishize masculinity. Hollywood cinema customarily bids the female subject to look at the male with her 'imagination' rather than with her eyes in order to disavow his castration and endow him with 'phallic sufficiency' (Silverman 1992: 8). These films depict 'ideal' female subjects who collude in the dominant fiction and refuse to recognize male lack, investing their belief in patently artificial images of male adequacy or the phallus as a signifier of desire. But Silverman also finds other films, both from Hollywood and elsewhere, that depict 'deviant' masculinities which both acknowledge and embrace castration, alterity, and specularity. Some of these 'deviant' masculinities say 'no' to power – a stance that implies reconciliation with the terms and conditions of all subjectivity, and therefore also with what has traditionally been designated as 'feminine'. This, too, Silverman claims, calls for urgent feminist investigation, for such a 'large-scale reconfiguration of male identification and desire would . . . permit female subjectivity to be lived differently than it is at present', as well as making 'null and void virtually everything else that commands general belief' (Silverman 1992: 2–3).

HISTORICAL TRAUMA

From postwar film noir to contemporary male melodramas, Hollywood has frequently dramatized crises of confidence in traditional masculinity and attempts at its recuperation. One example of feminist scholarship in this area, which has directly influenced Silverman's work, is Susan Jeffords's book *The Remasculinization of America: Gender and the Vietnam War* (1989). Jeffords's term 'remasculinization' implies that masculinity is in an endangered state – a state of emasculation – and in need of rejuvenation. She looks at how the discourse of war works to reconstruct conventional masculinity. Silverman, on the other hand, focuses on films where masculine power and privilege are renounced instead of reaffirmed, where masculine flaws and vulnerabilities are put on display rather than being concealed.

Silverman defines historical trauma as a historical event which makes a collective of men confront lack so intimately that it shatters the coherence of the male ego and reveals the abyss of lack that it conceals (Silverman 1992: 55). It leads to a temporary collapse of the penis/ phallus equation and other elements of the dominant fiction. Although this relation with lack is primarily psychic, a male subject is more likely to represent it to himself as anatomical deficiency – and this is how it is usually cinematically depicted.

'At those historical moments', Silverman writes, 'when the proto-typical male subject is unable to recognize "himself" within its conjuration of masculine sufficiency our society suffers from a profound sense of "ideological fatigue"' (Silverman 1992: 16). Such a moment was registered in Hollywood films produced in the immediate after-math of the Second World War, testifying to a crisis in traditional masculinity due to the trauma of that war and the subsequent recovery period. These films feature returning war veterans who bear psychic or physical wounds that mark them as deficient and render them unable to function smoothly in civilian life. The veterans no longer feel comfortable in the small towns where they grew up; everything seems changed and unfamiliar. They are made anxious by their apparent 'redundancy', finding their traditional functions taken over by other men or, more disturbingly, by women, whose mobilization on the home front during war showed to returning soldiers that society could manage quite well without them. These men, hitherto believed to be self-sufficient, now find themselves dependent on others.

In such films, the norms of sexual difference are unsettled. The standard 'boy gets girl' formula no longer applies: a female character acquires the narrative agency usually bestowed on the male character; and she is more insistently positioned as a spectator than he is (Silverman 1992: 52). Along with the collapse of faith in traditional masculinity, these films testify to a concomitant collapse in America's 'reality' in the immediate postwar period, a sense of 'ideological fatigue' induced by loss of belief in the family and small-town life as well as of the male subject (Silverman 1992: 54). In one of the films Silverman discusses, *The Best Years of Our Lives* (1946), three ex-servicemen return from war, one of them an amputee with an artificial claw hand. According to Silverman, this movie inverts the paradigm of the look: women are summoned to see the men's lack, rather than to display their own lack. They acknowledge the men's castration – they do not disavow it – and despite this, or rather because of it, they feel desire for the men, with all their psychic and physical wounds.

In Silverman's analysis, *The Best Years of Our Lives* brings the male subject face-to-face with castration, specularity, and alterity – all of which shatters the supports of the dominant fiction. Through its depiction of historical trauma, the film dramatizes the vulnerability of conventional masculinity and the wider dominant fiction. However, Silverman is not suggesting historical trauma as the solution to 'mass *méconnaissance*' nor as an agent of social transformation; rather, to show how conventional masculine certainties were destroyed as an inadvertent by-product of the Second World War, and to suggest that 'the typical male subject, like his female counterpart, might learn to live with lack' (Silverman 1992: 65).

It's A Wonderful Life (1946), another of Silverman's examples, resolves these issues in a way that reaffirms the dominant fiction, but not before registering the historical trauma. Under the strain of accomplishing this, the film pushes Hollywood conventions to the limit – it breaks the realist artifice and brings in '"heavenly" reinforcements' (Silverman 1992: 53). The desperate plight of George Bailey (James Stewart) comes to the attention of the heavenly Father, who sends a guardian angel, Clarence, down to earth to assist him. George is not a war veteran, but the war forms the backdrop of the entire film, although it is only shown briefly. George is conspicuously marked by lack – first, in the form of a physical deficiency, having been deaf in one ear ever since he saved his brother Harry's life by jumping into a freezing pool. Pronounced medically unfit for service, he stays in his hometown Bedford Falls during the war, while Harry becomes a heroic fighter pilot; and, in peacetime, the need to save the family business prevents him from realizing his desires to travel and escaping his hometown, which he hates.

In the flashback to George's childhood, Clarence is shown how George once stopped his drugstore employer from accidentally poisoning customers. Perturbed by the insufficiency of this particular father-figure, the young George takes a hint from an advert depicting 'a cigar-wielding patriarch', with the words 'Ask Dad. *He* knows' (Silverman 1992: 95). However, when he finds his father, he overhears him being called a failure by Potter, an unscrupulous businessman. George immediately defends his father: 'You're the biggest man in the whole town, bigger than him [Potter], bigger than everybody!' He tries to repair the disparity between the actual and Symbolic father, between the penis and the phallus, yet his identification with a 'weak' father actually highlights that gap.

Later, at the brink of suicide due to debt and his own sense of failure, George is given a chance – by divine grant – to see what the world would have been like had he never been born. He discovers that if he had not been there to save his brother, Harry would have died and never have saved thousands of lives during the war. If George had not sacrificed his own plans and not taken on his father's business, the town would have been engulfed by Potter's greedy enterprises. George's wife Mary would have become a lonely spinster and their children would not exist. George's non-existence appears to leave an irreparable 'hole' in the universe.

According to Silverman's analysis, however, the hole is actually in postwar male subjectivity, which the film strives to suture up. The movie heals the trauma by reassuring the average male subject that he is indispensable – not redundant, as feared – and adequate as paternal head of the family and leader of the community. Through his inter-mediary, Clarence, the omnipotent heavenly Father makes good the male subject's lack, restoring belief in male subjectivity, the family, and life in small-town America. The male subject is reintegrated into the reconstituted dominant fiction.

THE SCREEN AND THE GAZE

Among the films that Silverman explores in *Male Subjectivity at the Margins* are those by the gay filmmaker Rainer Werner Fassbinder. These films push the representation of marginal masculinities further still than postwar Hollywood. The following section addresses this in relation to Fassbinder's *Fear Eats the Soul* (1974), which deals with the love affair between a young Moroccan immigrant worker, Ali, and a white cleaning woman in her sixties, Emmi, and focuses on the hostile looks the couple face from others in 1970s German society.

While Mulvey stipulated a controlling, objectifying male gaze that reduces the female body to spectacle as the structuring force of narra-tive film, *Fear Eats the Soul* throws this notion of the gaze into question, not only because both male and female characters participate in the interplay of objectifying, aggressive stares but also because it is a male body – Ali's – that is the prime object of erotic spectacle. (Not coincidentally, the director's former lover, El Hedi ben Salem, plays Ali.) In her analysis, Silverman distinguishes between the gaze and the look. Following Lacan's *Seminar XI: the Four Fundamental Concepts*, she de-anthropomorphizes the gaze, arguing that it can never be 'at one' with human vision – the gaze is, rather, a function of light and Otherness. It arises from all sides, rather than from one viewer or group of viewers. All subjects, male and female, are subordinate to the gaze.

This is significantly different from the gaze as it has usually been theorized in feminist film theory. It might be helpful to designate Lacan's concept of the Gaze with a capital G, and to compare the relationship between the Gaze and the gaze – which feminist film theory designates as male – to that between the phallus and the penis. For example, the male voyeur may think he possesses the Gaze, which endows him with the power to control and objectify, yet the Gaze (like the phallus) is impossible to grasp. In the field of vision, no subject's 'gaze' is ever all-powerful or transcendent. The spectator is simultaneously part of the spectacle.

Unlike the Gaze, the gaze (with a small g) or what Silverman calls 'the look' comes from a subject or subjects; and, like the subject, it is marked by lack. In one scene in *Fear Eats the Soul*, for example, Emmi looks at Ali naked in the shower, the camera framing him in a mirror. 'You're very handsome, Ali', she utters regretfully, aware in comparison of her own lack of sexual appeal. The look may convey desire but in so doing it also conveys the looker's lack.

The Gaze oppresses and controls: it 'confirms and sustains the subject's identity', although it does not determine the form which that identity takes (Silverman 1992: 145). An individual can sadistically identify with the Gaze by projecting his or her own lack, insufficiency, or desire onto another. This is how the hostile looks work in *Fear Eats the Soul*. Characters try to enact the Gaze that controls and confirms identity. In cafés, pubs, and restaurants, Emmi and Ali are trapped by aggressive stares that confirm their status as outsiders.

There are some scenes in the film, however, that are not marked by oppressive looks, such as those in the bar owner Barbara's flat, where Ali escapes when his relationship with Emmi starts to disintegrate. In one famous shot, Barbara is shown behind Ali, clasping his torso in desire. In another sequence, the camera turns from a shot of Barbara in the mirror to a long shot of Ali undressing through the doorway. Silverman resists the impulse to label this 'the Female Gaze', with the male body figuring as the 'object of desire', for neither the male nor the female subject can possess the Gaze as such.

Instead, she suggests that in these scenes, the Gaze is 'redefined through its alignment with Barbara's desiring and accepting look' (Silverman 1992: 143). Up to this point, through long shots and long takes, the camera has assured that we largely see Ali (and Emmi) as others see them, in an objectifying manner. Fassbinder's technical choices deliberately force viewers to feel their complicity with the prejudiced characters who stare at the couple, finding Emmi 'too old' and Ali 'too black'. However, in scenes in Barbara's flat, the audience is encouraged to view Ali differently. It is as if a new filter or 'screen' has been placed in the path of our look.

In *The Four Fundamental Concepts of Psychoanalysis*, Lacan refers to the 'screen' as the image, or set of images, that predetermines how any subject of representation is viewed (Lacan 1994: 107). Extending the cultural implications, Silverman characterizes the 'screen' as the 'culturally generated' repertoire of images, which defines us in relation to sex, race, age, class, and nationality (Silverman 1992: 150). It is a grid of cultural representations through which we are trained to see and through which we ourselves are seen. When they look upon Ali, the majority of the characters in the film only see what the dominant cultural screen of race in 1970s Germany allows them to see, namely, 'the very "picture" of social and sexual marginality' (Silverman 1992: 145). If the Gaze is like an imaginary camera, as Lacan suggests, then the screen is what decides *how* the subject will be 'photographed'. Only forms of identity mandated by the dominant fiction will enter visibility. All the rest – the subjects not ratified by the dominant fiction – will be screened out.

It is, however, possible to manipulate the screen, as Fassbinder does in these scenes. In her later book *Threshold of the Visible World* (1996) Silverman explores how films can offer images of bodies despised and marginalized by dominant cultural representations and make them attractive. Films have the ability to confer ideality to subjects – this does not necessarily put them in thrall to the dominant fiction but can enable them to defy it. All this gives further force to her claim, in *Male Subjectivity at the Margins*, that the screen – not the gaze – is the political arena where cultural representations should be contested and fought. Crucially, it offers feminist film theory a way of moving beyond the critique of dominant representations by suggesting how things can be changed – by playing with the screen or creating new relationships between the look and the screen. This is not a matter of providing 'positive images' of women, blacks, gays, and other marginalized groups – such images work to 'resubstantialize' and 'essentialize' identity while Silverman's point is precisely to question it.

MALE MASOCHISM

Silverman traces her own 'obsession' with male subjectivity as lacking or impaired to watching and writing about Liliana Cavani's film *Night Porter* (1974) (Silverman 1988: 234). As mentioned in Chapter 3, Cavani's films are marked by the director's strong identification with her male protagonists. Moreover, all Cavani's protagonists 'occupy subject-positions which are more classically "feminine" than "masculine" . . . demanding of them passivity, suffering and renunciation' (Silverman 1988: 219). They demonstrate the allure of masochism for male characters.

In 'Masochism and Subjectivity', the article where she discusses *Night Porter*, Silverman argues that the experience of instinctual pain is essential to the child's process of gaining subjectivity and entering the Symbolic Order. That experience is incurred through the child's losses – its separation from the mother's breast and other objects that it felt intimately as part of its own being. The Oedipal moment, which involves further loss, conceals these earlier losses from us. Moreover, in becoming a subject, the child is subjected to an Order which is much bigger than it and which it can never hope to master. All this indicates that cultural gain or pleasure *depends* on instinctual renunciation or pain, underlining the role of masochism – i.e. pleasure in powerlessness and pain – in the constitution of subjectivity.

According to Silverman, 'texts provide pleasure to the degree that they reposition us culturally; to the extent that they oblige us to re-enact those moments of loss and false recovery by which we are constituted as subjects; insofar as they master us' (Silverman 1980: 3). The re-enactment of the castration crisis and Oedipus Complex are only 'the most obvious examples' of these painful situations. But, as we have already seen in numerous filmic examples, the male subject tends to displace his own feelings of loss and lack onto women. The same happens with masochism – although common to all subjectivity, it is generally regarded as a female condition. We are all familiar with the stereotype of masochistic femininity – of passive and suffering women. In most cultural texts, women, rather than men, are depicted in passive positions and men, rather than women, act as aggressors. However, Silverman contends that, when watching a film where a female character occupies the passive position, the male viewer 'enacts, through displacement, the compulsory narrative of loss and recovery':

> It is always the victim – the figure who occupies the passive position – who is really the focus of attention, and whose subjugation the subject (whether male or female) experiences as a pleasurable repetition of his/her own history. Indeed I would go so far as to say that the fascination of the sadistic point of view is merely that it provides the best vantage point from which to watch the masochistic story unfold.
>
> (Silverman 1980: 5)

This can be seen in the story of *Night Porter*, which portrays a relationship between a Nazi photographer, Max (Dirk Bogarde), and a concentration camp inmate, Lucia (Charlotte Rampling), who becomes his favourite 'model'. The film appears to set up the classic binary between the male-sadist-voyeur and female-masochist-exhibitionist. However, in Silverman's reading, what fascinates Max is not his own cruelty, but Lucia's pain, with which he actually identifies (Silverman 1980: 5). The couple resume their relationship when they are reunited in a hotel where Max works as a night porter, many years after the war. 'Tell me what to do', Max asks Lucia, begging to assume the masochistic role. They go into hiding from other undercover Nazis, who seek to eliminate surviving witnesses. Their situation forces Max to divest himself of the power and privilege (i.e. of the phallus) that being male confers on him. In his sadomasochistic exchange with Lucia, he ritually submits to pain, to what has traditionally been *her* position: he steps over the cultural boundary that divides male from female subjectivity.

Freud outlined three different forms of masochism: first, there is erotogenic masochism (pleasure in pain), which forms the 'corporeal basis' of the other two categories, moral masochism (a desire to be punished for 'sins') and feminine masochism (associated with fantasies of being bound and beaten) (Silverman 1992: 188). Feminine masochism is so called because it places the sufferer in a position culturally constructed as feminine. As we have seen, masochism structures both male and female subjectivity, but it is only in relation to female subjectivity that it can be 'safely acknowledged'. So Silverman argues that it is actually a male disorder, for only in men does it appear as being abnormal. The male subject cannot admit his masochism without associating himself with femininity and raising doubts about his masculinity (Silverman 1992: 190). For Silverman, therefore, male masochism in its feminine form has a radical potential: not only does it overturn the sex/gender system, it renounces phallic identification. In her words, 'the male masochist magnifies the losses and divisions upon which cultural identity is based, refusing to be sutured or recompensed. In short, he radiates a negativity inimical to the social order' (Silverman 1992: 206).

The French philosopher Gilles Deleuze (1925–95) has offered another very influential account of masochism in 'Coldness and Cruelty', an essay originally published in 1967. Deleuze points to the role of the mother as the torturer in masochistic fantasy. In his account, the masochist invites the mother to beat or dominate him, thus transferring the father's power and authority to her. In other words, the masochist identifies the mother with the Law and expels the father from the Symbolic Order. Deleuze claims that 'what is beaten, humiliated and ridiculed' in the masochist is 'the image and the likeness of the father' (Deleuze 1997: 66). In this way, 'the masochist . . . liberates himself in preparation for a rebirth in which the father will have no part'.

Silverman finds Deleuze's account of masochism sympathetic to her own. This is not surprising because his image of a male subjectivity 'ruining' its paternal legacy and remaking the Symbolic Order is similar to the utopian fantasy articulated in her own writing. However, the feminist critic Tania Modleski has highlighted problems in this theory of masochism in her book *Feminism Without Women* (1991). She declares that, while appearing to surrender his authority, the male masochist actually maintains it in another form – after all, he is the one who assigns to the woman her new, powerful role – and 'no necessary shift in power dynamics accompanies such a move' (Modleski 1991: 74).

The ability to renounce power, as the male masochists do in Silverman and Deleuze's scenarios, can be seen as a 'luxury' belonging to those already empowered (Modleski 1991: 149). However,

Silverman says she does not want to hold up feminine masochism as 'the model for a radically reconstituted male subjectivity' – 'masochism in all its guises is as much a product of the existing symbolic order as a reaction against it' (Silverman 1992: 213). But she also concludes that if, in the attempt to depose him, the Symbolic Father remains the fantasy's hidden reference point, 'it is also the case that the son does not . . . manifest any desire to fill his boots' (Silverman 1992: 212), indicating that the fantasy has a cultural relevance beyond her own, personal captivation by its image.

SUMMARY

This chapter has focused on Silverman's feminist intervention into the area of 'masculinity in crisis'. She reveals the notion of 'traditional' masculinity as an ideological construction based on an imaginary equation between the penis and the phallus. This ideology of masculinity is a key support for the 'dominant fiction' – the repertoire of images through which a society establishes consensus about its 'reality'. Loss of belief in the notion of traditional masculinity can shake faith in the entire dominant fiction, as testified by some postwar Hollywood films.

'Deviant' ('non-phallic') or marginal masculinities occupy the domain of the culturally 'feminine'. So Silverman contends that any changes in conceptions of masculinity are bound to impact on the way female subjectivity is lived and perceived. In a discussion of Fassbinder's films, she extends her critique to the gaze, insisting that it is impossible for anyone to obtain the kind of visual power that feminist theorists have ascribed to the male gaze, just as it is impossible for anyone to possess the phallus. Finally, in the image of the male subject renouncing his privilege and power, the chapter finds the source of Silverman's fascination with 'marginal' male subjectivity. Through this utopian fantasy, Silverman challenges the cultural equation that places men on the side of mastery, voyeurism, and sadism, and women on the side of passivity, exhibitionism, and masochism.

AFTER MULVEY, SILVERMAN, DE LAURETIS, AND CREED

Although other pioneers such as Claire Johnston helped to formulate the debates, it was really Mulvey who, with her concept of the male gaze, defined their terms and set into motion a specific agenda. Arguing that narrative cinema assumes a masculinized spectator, whose desiring gaze takes the female as its object, she emphasized the way that sexual difference is articulated in structures of looking, altering our whole approach not only to film but across the gamut of visual culture. This makes her not simply the author of a particular text, 'Visual Pleasure and Narrative Cinema', but the generator of an entire discourse: 'in this respect', as the film theorist D.N. Rodowick has remarked, 'we all owe a great debt to the work of Laura Mulvey' (Rodowick 1989: 274).

As Film Studies was a relatively young discipline in the 1970s, it was particularly receptive to new ideas, including feminist film theory, and Mulvey's essay quickly attained the status of a 'classic'. The danger of this almost-immediate adoption of feminist ideas within film theory, however, is that such ideas simply become part of the establishment. Nonetheless, other feminist film theorists have challenged and refined Mulvey's arguments. Apart from Mulvey herself, this book has focused on Kaja Silverman, Teresa de Lauretis, and Barbara Creed, all of whom have helped to define new areas of inquiry within feminist film theory, offering their own array of valuable critical tools. Their work has also been expanded by their contemporaries, both within the field of film theory and beyond. In her later work, Mulvey herself acknowledges the influence of de Lauretis, Silverman, and Creed, as well as paying tribute to other feminist film theorists who have contributed to the field, including Mary Ann Doane, E. Ann Kaplan, and Tania Modleski (Mulvey 1996: xii, 26; Mulvey 1998a: 31n8). This concluding chapter underlines the usefulness of all the feminist film theorists' insights to contemporary film and theory, and highlights some of their recent work.

As we have seen throughout this book, psychoanalysis has been vital to feminist film theory's intellectual development. Yet, the use of psychoanalysis has by no means met with unanimous approval. Psychoanalytic feminist film theorists have often been criticized for deploying abstract and over-generalized psychoanalytic paradigms. The need for them to address other differences than the sexual difference between men and women has been reiterated many times, often with an appeal to 'history' or the 'real' experience of women watching films. But although it is easy to say that feminist theory must account for differences among women, such as those of race, class, and sexuality, it is much harder to carry it out – especially in a way that acknowledges the complex relations between all these differences.

In any case, the work of theorists such as de Lauretis and Silverman can hardly be described as universalizing. Together with the theoretical agenda she inaugurated under the rubric of 'queer theory', de Lauretis's concept of the technology of gender resituates men and women in relation to diverse social power strategies, enabling insights into how gender coalesces with other forms of oppression. As an Italian émigré to the US, she is especially motivated to situate herself, both culturally and theoretically, in her writing and this has undoubtedly shaped her interest in representing concerns of difference and specificity. Similarly, Creed's position as an Australian theorist, while located within the Western feminist theory establishment, has also prompted her to articulate an increasingly culturally-situated perspective in her work, as can be seen by comparing *The Monstrous-Feminine*, her major contribution to the study of the horror genre, with her later book *Media Matrix*, which extends her insights into the structures of horror to a multitude of postmodern media.

In her powerful critique of how the term 'the gaze' has been used in feminist film theory, Silverman undermines the usual binary between spectator and spectacle. For her, the problem of narrative cinema is not that men desire women, and purportedly express this through 'the gaze', but that male (and female) subjects identify with an objectifying, controlling gaze that displaces lack onto women. She argues that, rather than the gaze, the arena of cultural contestation should be the screen, a Lacanian concept that she reinvents as the culturally-changing repertoire of images through which we see and are seen. Her writings on marginal male subjectivity, furthermore, call into question the abstract, generalized category of 'man' hitherto constructed in feminist discourse. Perhaps most significantly, her work in this area demonstrates that feminism is not just the concern of women; as we have seen in Chapter 7, feminism's contestations of the 'dominant fiction' can radically alter – for the better – the entire values and conditions under which both male and female subjectivities are currently lived.

The key concepts that these theorists discuss are in many ways no less pertinent and fraught with complexity than when they were first placed on the agenda. From this perspective, the unrealized critical potential of their work, especially on the female voice, the technologies of gender, queering desire, and masculinity in crisis has yet to be mined. But what of the other future areas of inquiry for feminist film theory? Most feminist film theory of the last three decades has been formulated in relation to Hollywood, which has been conceived as the 'dominant cinema', a primary institution through which patriarchal ideology is reproduced (Mulvey's article on the Senegalese film *Xala* [1975] is one of the relatively few exceptions; see Mulvey 1996). In order to tackle the most urgent issues in the medium today, however, feminist film theory increasingly needs to look beyond Hollywood and to engage with the broader traditions of international filmmaking. Although Hollywood is the dominant cinema in most parts of the world, it is not so universally (for example, Bollywood reigns in South Asia) while concepts of gender, genre, narrative, and stardom – all of which feminist film theory has traditionally conceived in terms of Hollywood models – necessarily differ worldwide. The changing conditions under which audiences view films, no longer always collectively but often at home on video or DVD, also call for new theories of spectatorship and reflections on the future of cinema – and this is the topic of Mulvey's newest book *Death 24 × a Second* (2005).

Here, Mulvey reconsiders 'Visual Pleasure and Narrative Cinema' in the light of new technologies, which, she argues, can produce new modes of spectatorship, including 'pensive' and 'possessive' spectators.

For example, watching films on video or DVD enables the flow of the film to be halted and favourite images or scenes to be repeated. This can create a 'cinema of delay', an aesthetic of stillness, and a weakening of cause-and-effect narrative links not unlike the effects produced by avant-garde films, but this time such pleasures are available not only for an elite but to any user of these new technologies. Rather than being absorbed into vicarious identification with his or her screen surrogates, the spectator actually has control of the film and is able to possess images that were previously elusive. Watching classical Hollywood films on DVD, therefore, gives rise to viewing practices that are totally different from those imagined at the time of their making.

It must be recognized that the extension of feminist film theories fostered in the West (and in relation to Western film-texts) to the burgeoning area of 'world cinema' does not simply ratify those theories by 'proving' their 'universal' applicability, but rather offers further opportunities for the theories to be interrogated and refined through encounters with different cultural contexts. In fact, it poses new challenges to any claim to universality by insisting on the historical particularities of patriarchy in different parts of the world.

We can see this in Mulvey's work on Iranian cinema, particularly on Abbas Kiarostami, whose film *Through the Olive Trees* she recalls first seeing in 1996:

> For me, as a film theorist, Kiarostami's film seemed to have more in common with the avant-garde than with art cinema, while his way of storytelling, shooting and dealing with cinematic reality touched on ideas familiar to film theory but defied any expected aesthetic and analytic framework.
>
> (Mulvey 1998b: 24)

Kiarostami's films are made under the strict censorship of an Islamic republic. These censorship codes, put into place in 1982 (three years after the Iranian Revolution, when the current regime came to power), observe the rules of women's modesty, known as *hejab*. Such notions of modesty define daily social interactions between men and women as well as what can be represented in cinema. *Hejab* requires women to veil themselves before any man who is not a close relative. It marks women out from men and – as the cultural critic Hamid Naficy remarks in his study of veiling – 'purportedly protects them from the male gaze' (Naficy 1994: 140). However, as Mulvey acknowledges, Islamic customs of veiling imply a different understanding of the gaze from Western feminist theories of voyeurism (Mulvey 2002: 259). Within Iranian cinema, a very specific 'aesthetics and grammar of vision and veiling' has evolved that traditionally forbids close-ups of women and direct exchange of desiring looks between the sexes (Naficy 1994: 132). The audience, moreover, cannot have the illusion that they are private voyeurs as Western viewers do, because the actors on-screen observe the same rules of modesty as they would in public – even in intimate, bedroom screens.

Although such a regime would appear to be 'at odds' with her feminist commitment, Mulvey notes a strange coincidence between the results of this censorship and the problems that she and others have highlighted about the cinema's representation of women. Moreover, despite – or perhaps rather because of – its censorship, Iran has produced an innovative cinema where conventional ways of seeing are challenged. For example, the grammar of veiling leads Iranian films to subvert the system of suture, where viewers are 'stitched' into the narrative flow through point-of-view and the shot/reverse-shot, which conveys an exchange of looks. Instead, Iranian films have been forced to opt for other styles and techniques such as long shots and the averted or fleeting look.

These issues are dramatized in *Through the Olive Trees*, which takes the form of a film-within-a-film, the inset film dramatizing the relationship between a newly-wed couple. Matters are complicated by the fact that the actor playing the husband, Hossein, is in love with the actress playing his wife and has asked to marry her in real life but has been rejected by her family. During the course of the film, he renews his pursuit, later insisting to Tahereh that she had once returned his look. However, according to Mulvey, in the scene as shown in flashback to the audience, 'the camera registers Hossein's intense gaze but gives no indication of Tahereh's look'. For her, Tahereh's unseen look makes explicit women's problematic status and representation, allowing this 'outstanding blindspot of Islamic culture' to 'make a tentative step on to the screen' (Mulvey 2005: 139–40).

Cross-cultural film criticism has emerged as one of the most exciting areas of feminist film theory's current impact, including in the work of Chinese-American theorist Rey Chow, who adapts the concept of the gaze in her book *Primitive Passions* (1995), which both contests and reworks the insights of feminist and other Western theories. The gaze of the West at non-Western people has often been characterized in terms of scopophilia, which reduces non-Westerners to a 'passive, objectified, fetishized status', as often seen in films about 'the Orient' and tourist brochures (Chow 1995: 12). Chow argues, however, that such claims about the Western gaze lock 'West' and 'East' into a spectator/exhibit relationship, which overlooks 'the fact that "the East," too, is a spectator who is equally caught up in the dialectic of seeing' (Chow 1995: 12–13). In the work of Chinese filmmaker Zhang Yimou, who is often accused of pandering to Western 'tastes', it is clear that Easterners themselves are capable of using the film medium to fantasize about the Orient and its people.

Chow also demonstrates the broad applicability of Silverman's work on the female voice to another Chinese film, Chen Kaige's *Yellow Earth* (1984), where the voice of the heroine Cuiqiao inhabits an interior space in the diegesis, heard within a recording within the film. In Chapter 3, we saw how Silverman strives to relocate the female voice within the signifying practices of the Symbolic Order. Without wanting to ignore 'the lessons we have learned from Western feminism', Chow nonetheless cautions that 'the assertion of woman's rise to speech would be a false approach to the problems raised in this context' (Chow 1995: 97). Yet, she also analyzes films such as *King of the Children* (1987), which more fully bear out Silverman's other work on male subjectivity; such films, Chow writes, reverse the Hollywood paradigm in making the male look the bearer of lack and placing it in the classically 'feminine' passive position, due to the 'symbolic castration, or cultural violence, which is particularly germane to the understanding of the contemporary Chinese situation' (Chow 1995: 229n15).

Kyung Hyun Kim's *The Remasculinization of Korean Cinema* (2004) draws on Silverman's writings on male subjectivity as part of its main theoretical framework, declaring that its use of Western psychoanalytic terms is not intended 'to validate theory but to better elucidate Korean films that have become increasingly "Westernized"' (Kim 2004: x). It deals with themes of masochism, emasculation, and alienation of male characters in South Korean films made in the aftermath of the Korean War and the subsequent military dictatorships. Many of the characters from films of the 1980s, for example, are 'either physically handicapped or psychologically traumatized (sometimes both)', figuring as emblems of 'the period's frustration when protest against the military government was disallowed' (Kim 2004:5). Male lack became a key feature of postwar films and was 'located in every field imaginable: of the accoutrements of male power in sexual potency, paternal authority, communal function, historical legitimacy, and professional worth' (Kim 2004: 12). Kim also charts the recuperation of male subjectivity in films of the post-authoritarian period, which 'sought to reorient the subject back on its track into the Lacanian Symbolic where language could be reacquired, the Name of the Father reissued, and castration anxiety disavowed' (Kim 2004: 12).

This book hopes to have shown that despite the prevailing belief that both film theory, including feminist film theory, and feminism have come to an end, this is far from the case. Such a belief is not only unfounded but also dangerous, for it cuts off the present generation from the earlier generation's insights – a wilful forgetting of the past that entails the loss not only of the history of feminist activism, and of awareness of its many as yet unfinished aims, but also of feminist film theory's intellectual history, which evolved through a dialogue with semiotics, Marxism, and psychoanalysis. Hence this book has asserted the importance of theory, not just activism, to the feminist project.

Rather than simply dismissing these traditions, any radically new developments in the field must acknowledge them, as some new works that adopt an alternative theoretical framework derived from the philosopher Gilles Deleuze have done (see Jayamanne 1995; Rodowick 2000; Pisters 2003). While it is not surprising that, after thirty years of psychoanalytic feminist film theory, some contemporary theorists are searching for new conceptual paradigms, the best new approaches will necessarily stress their links with, as well as their differences from, the old models. Psychoanalytic feminism will remain important for the future of film theory and feminism not simply as an orthodoxy to be challenged but as a vital historical and intellectual formation.

Many people assume we are more 'progressive' about gender issues now than we ever have been in the past, implying a linear view of history. However, as the backlashes against feminism show, societies have a tendency to move back as well as forward. This makes re-reading the work of feminist theorists such as Mulvey, de Lauretis, Silverman, and Creed more urgent than ever. Their work forms a solidly committed basis for new explorations that may once again transform the ways in which film as a medium is understood, inspiring theoretical reflection about where we are now and the many feminist battles that are not over but remain to be fought.

FURTHER READING

This section lists the main works by Mulvey, Silverman, de Lauretis, and Creed that have been discussed in the book, as well as some other key works of feminist theory and critical overviews. As feminist film theory is an enormous field, this list concentrates on some of the most influential works of the 1980s and 1990s, but is necessarily selective. There are also plenty of 'readers' and anthologies of feminist film theory, some of which are listed here, that make the key and influential essays easy to access. If different from the editions used, original publication dates are given in square brackets.

WORKS BY MULVEY, SILVERMAN, DE LAURETIS, AND CREED

Mulvey, Laura (1989) *Visual and Other Pleasures*, Basingstoke: Macmillan.
This collection gathers together articles Mulvey wrote between 1971 and 1986, including her celebrated 'Visual Pleasure and Narrative Cinema' [1975]. The book is divided into sections, with titles such as 'Iconoclasm', 'Melodrama', and 'Avant-Garde', allowing the reader to follow Mulvey's intellectual trajectory from her involvement in the Women's Liberation Movement and avant-garde practice through to her renewed interest in melodrama and narrative. Essays such as 'The Spectacle is Vulnerable: Miss World, 1970' (co-written with Margarita

Jimenez) and the introduction in which she reflects on the feminist movement and on how she turned her own love of Hollywood film into 'passionate detachment' offer a valuable background for her most famous essay which has had, she remarks, a tendency to float free of its contexts in the aftermath of the constant references to it (Mulvey 1989a: vii). *Visual and Other Pleasures* provides a good starting point for a consideration of her work.

Mulvey, Laura (1996) *Fetishism and Curiosity*, London: BFI.

Here, Mulvey revisits many of her earlier concerns, including fetishism, narrative, the work of Jean-Luc Godard, and Douglas Sirk's melodramas, this time emphasizing a Marxist approach and a historical dimension that was less apparent in her previous discussions of such topics. In the book, she formulates a theory of 'curiosity' – the spectator's drive to know, interpret, and understand, which forms a dialectical relationship with the compulsions of fetishism that she had outlined earlier. The collection also contains a reprint of 'The Carapace That Failed', her essay on the Sengalese film *Xala* (1975), which marked the start of her interest in world cinemas, as well as very readable and thought-provoking essays (influenced by Teresa de Lauretis) on Oedipal narrative structures in *Citizen Kane* (1941) and *Blue Velvet* (1986).

Mulvey, Laura (2005) *Death 24 × a Second: Stillness and the Moving Image*, London: Reaktion Books.

This book explores new modes of spectatorship arising in the wake of new production and distribution technologies – how watching films on DVD, for example, can produce 'pensive' or 'possessive' spectators quite unlike the kind of spectator implied by classical Hollywood film. It contains a chapter on the Iranian director Abbas Kiarostami, whose films also encourage new ways of seeing.

Silverman, Kaja (1983) *The Subject of Semiotics*, New York: Oxford University Press.

This book provides an advanced introduction to semiotic and psychoanalytic theory. It contains, in embryonic form, the theoretical arguments that Silverman develops in her subsequent books. It also presents her theory of suture, which she illustrates very effectively with *Psycho* (1960).

Silverman, Kaja (1988) *The Acoustic Mirror: The Female Voice in Psychoanalysis and Cinema*, Bloomington: Indiana University Press.

This study of how sexual difference is constructed in film sound-tracks argues that the female voice is traditionally deprived of author-itative speech and that, in this respect, classical cinema shares the same paradigm as most psychoanalytic theory, which similarly consigns the female voice to a place outside the Symbolic. It is a lucid yet challeng-ing book, which supports its claims with convincing film analyses.

Silverman, Kaja (1992) *Male Subjectivity at the Margins*, New York: Routledge.

This is another theoretically detailed and complex work, which provides an account of 'marginal' masculinities and their ability to threaten or undermine society's dominant ideologies. The book collects together, in a revised form, a number of essays on male subjectivity that Silverman wrote earlier, and adds new material on male maso-chism and gay sexuality, particularly in relation to Fassbinder's cinema.

De Lauretis, Teresa (1984) *Alice Doesn't: Feminism, Semiotics, Cinema*, Bloomington: Indiana University Press.

In this engaging and complex work, de Lauretis tracks the narrative image of 'Woman' through myth, psychoanalytic theory, and avant-garde and narrative film. Through readings of films such as *Rebecca* (1940) and *Vertigo* (1958), she demonstrates the techniques through which narrative and cinema solicit women's consent and attempt to seduce them into femininity.

De Lauretis, Teresa (1987) *Technologies of Gender: Essays on Theory, Film, and Fiction*, Bloomington: Indiana University Press.

This essay collection brings together a number of de Lauretis's important essays, including 'The Technology of Gender' and her writ-ings on women's cinema, 'Strategies of Coherence: Narrative Cinema, Feminist Poetics, and Yvonne Rainer', and 'Rethinking Women's Cinema'. It sets out her ongoing concerns about the non-coincidence between Woman and women as well as explaining her adaptation of Foucault's theories. This is probably the best starting point for those who are new to de Lauretis's work.

De Lauretis, Teresa (1994) *The Practice of Love: Lesbian Sexuality and Perverse Desire*, Bloomington: Indiana University Press.

This book presents a thorough critique of feminist and psychoana-lytic theories of lesbian sexuality. It offers de Lauretis's own, intricate account of lesbian desire, based on analyses of lesbian film and fiction, an unorthodox reading of Freud's theory of fetishism, and her own self-analysis – an important contribution to queer theory.

Creed, Barbara (2001) [1993] The Monstrous-Feminine: Film, Feminism, Psychoanalysis, London: Routledge.

This imaginative account of the horror film renders complex arguments in a fairly accessible fashion. The first part of the book provides an outline of Kristeva's theory of abjection, which Creed uses to elaborate structures of horror and female monstrosity in films such as The Exorcist (1973), Alien (1979), and The Hunger (1983). The second part takes issue with a number of psychoanalytic theories, presenting the argument that it is the powerful, castrating woman, rather than the castrated woman, that provides the real image of film horror.

Creed, Barbara (2003) Media Matrix: Sexing the New Reality, Sydney: Allen and Unwin.

This accessible book surveys a diverse range of contemporary media, from reality television to women's romances and cybersex, combining psychoanalytic theories with an 'active audience' Cultural Studies methodology. It offers a number of interesting insights, especially into the phenomenon of 'crisis TV'.

Creed, Barbara (2005) Phallic Panic: Film, Horror and the Primal Uncanny, Manchester: Manchester University Press.

A study of male monsters in the horror film, which is a companion piece to The Monstrous-Feminine.

SOME OTHER KEY WORKS OF FEMINIST FILM THEORY

Clover, Carol (1992) Men, Women and Chain Saws: Gender in the Modern Horror Film, London: BFI.

This provides an alternative account of the horror genre, highlighting the transgender identification between male spectators and the figure of the Final Girl in the slasher film.

Doane, Mary Ann (1987) The Desire to Desire: The Woman's Film of the 1940s, Bloomington: Indiana University Press.

This study of the 1940s woman's film genre focuses on its attempt to delineate a place for the female spectator and to represent female subjectivity. Doane argues that such films repeatedly suggest a failure or inadequacy in the woman's endeavour to appropriate the gaze and her naive tendency to mistake the represented image for reality.

Doane, Mary Ann (1991) *Femmes Fatales: Feminism, Film Theory, Psychoanalysis*, New York: Routledge.

This study explores the femme fatale as an emblem of fears and anxieties of sexual difference as well as of issues about the instability of knowledge, vision, and agency. It contains Doane's influential essay 'Film and the Masquerade: Theorizing the Female Spectator', originally published in 1982, and a number of other important essays including 'Dark Continents: Epistemologies of Racial and Sexual Difference in Psychoanalysis and Cinema', where she considers the role of Freud's trope of woman as a dark continent in connection with the elision of race in feminist accounts of sexual difference.

hooks, bell (1992) *Black Looks: Race and Representation*, London: Turnaround.

This book considers representation as a crucial arena of political struggle for black people, articulating the desire to see blackness differently from the dominant ways of seeing. This struggle involves 'de-colonizing' the gaze from white supremacist images, through which black people learn to internalize racism. Several of the essays, including one entitled 'The Oppositional Gaze', deal with spectatorship.

Kuhn, Annette (1994) [1982] *Women's Pictures: Feminism and Cinema*, London: Verso.

This book explores the fraught relationships between feminist film theory, 'women's films', and feminist film practice. To negotiate these relationships, Kuhn offers the notion of the 'feminine' text, which is feminist insofar as it challenges the dominant modes of representation.

Williams, Linda (1999) [1989] *Hard Core: Power, Pleasure, and the 'Frenzy of the Visible'*, Berkeley: University of California Press.

This book explores the genre of film pornography. However, unlike anti-pornography feminists, Williams takes a non-condemnatory approach, viewing the genre not as a total objectification of the female body for male desire but as a site of varied discourses about sexuality in which hierarchies of male/female, sadist/masochist, and subject/object are often broken down.

ANTHOLOGIES OF FEMINIST FILM THEORY

Erens, Patricia (ed.) (1990) *Issues in Feminist Film Criticism*, Bloomington: Indiana University Press.

This anthology of essays encompasses a diverse range of critical approaches, with sections on 'Women and Representation', 'Rereading Hollywood Films', 'Feminist Filmmaking,' and 'Assessing Films Directed by Women', each prefaced by a helpful critical overview by Erens.

Grant, Barry (ed.) (1996) *Dread of Difference: Gender and the Horror Film*, Austin: University of Texas.

This contains a number of important feminist essays on the horror film, including Linda Williams's 'When a Woman Looks' [1983], Creed's 'Horror and Monstrous-Feminine: An Imaginary Abjection' [1986], and Clover's 'Her Body, Himself: Gender in the Slasher Film' [1987].

Kaplan, E. Ann (ed.) (2000) *Feminism and Film*, Oxford: Oxford University Press.

An excellent collection, with sections named after historical 'phases' of feminist film theory: 'Phase I. Pioneers and Classics' (including essays by Johnston, Mulvey, and Silverman), 'Phase II. Critiques of Phase I Theories: New Methods', 'Phase III. Race, Sexuality, and Postmodernism', and 'Phase IV. Spectatorship, Ethnicity, and Melodrama'.

Thornham, Sue (ed.) (1999) *Feminist Film Theory: A Reader*, Edinburgh: Edinburgh University Press.

Another useful anthology of essays, which serves as a companion to Thornham's book *Passionate Detachments* (see below).

SECONDARY READING

McCabe, Janet (2004) *Feminist Film Studies: Writing the Woman Into Cinema*, London: Wallflower Press.

This provides a broad overview of feminist film studies.

Smelik, Anneke (2004) [1999], 'Feminist Film Theory', in (ed.) Pam Cook and Mieke Bernink (eds) *The Cinema Book*, London: BFI.

This is probably the most succinct account of feminist film theory currently available.

Thornham, Sue (1997) *Passionate Detachments: An Introduction to Feminist Film Theory*, London: Arnold.

Like Thornham's edited collection of feminist film theory, this is a useful book, providing a detailed exposition of particular theoretical positions. However it does, to some extent, presuppose a reader who is already familiar with psychoanalytic theory and the other main debates.

WORKS CITED

If different from the dates of the editions used, original dates of publication have been given in square brackets.

Althusser, Louis (1999) [1970] 'Ideology and Ideological State Apparatuses (Notes Towards an Investigation)', in Slavoj Žižek (ed.) *Mapping Ideology*, London: Verso.

Ang, Ien (1991) [1985] *Watching Dallas: Soap Opera and the Melodramatic Imagination*, London: Routledge.

Barthes, Roland (1977) [1968] 'The Death of the Author', in *Image Music Text*, trans. Stephen Heath, London: Fontana.

—— (1993) [1957] *Mythologies*, London: Vintage.

Baudrillard, Jean (2002) *The Spirit of Terrorism*, London: Verso.

Beauvoir, Simone de (1993) [1949] *The Second Sex*, trans. H.M. Parshley, London: David Campbell.

Beh, Siew-Hwa and Salyer, Saunie (1972a) 'Overview', *Women and Film* 1: 3–6.

—— (1972b) 'A Note from the Editors', *Women and Film* 2: 3.

Brunsdon, Charlotte (1992) [1985] 'Text and Audience', in Ellen Seiter, Hans Borchers, Gabriele Kretzner, and Eva-Maria Warth (eds) *Remote Control: Television, Audiences, and Cultural Power*, London: Routledge.

Chow, Rey (1995) *Primitive Passions: Visuality, Sexuality, Ethnography, and Contemporary Chinese Cinema*, New York: Columbia University Press.

Clover, Carol (1996) [1987] 'Her Body, Himself: Gender in the Slasher Film', in Barry Keith Grant (ed.) *The Dread of Difference*, Austin: University of Texas Press.

Cohan, Steven and Hark, Ina Rae (1996) [1993] *Screening the Male: Exploring Masculinities in Hollywood Cinema*, London: Routledge.

Comolli, Jean-Luc and Narboni, Jean (1999) [1969] 'Cinema/Ideology/Criticism', in Leo Braudy and Marshall Cohen (eds) *Film Theory and Criticism*, Oxford: Oxford University Press.

Cook, Pam and Johnston, Claire (1990) [1974] 'The Place of Woman in the Cinema of Raoul Walsh', in Patricia Erens (ed.) *Issues in Feminist Film Criticism*, Bloomington: Indiana University Press.

Cowie, Elizabeth (1984) 'Fantasia', *m/f* 9: 71–105.

Creed, Barbara (1987) 'Feminist Film Theory: Reading the Text', in Annette Blonkski, Barbara Creed, and Freda Freiberg (eds) *Don't Shoot Darling! Women's Independent Filmmaking in Australia*, Richmond: Greenhouse Publications.

—— (2001) [1993] *The Monstrous-Feminine: Film, Feminism, Psycho-analysis*, London: Routledge.

—— (2003) *Media Matrix: Sexing the New Reality*, Sydney: Allen and Unwin.

—— (2005) *Phallic Panic: Film, Horror and the Primal Uncanny*, Manchester: Manchester University Press.

Dadoun, Roger (1989) [1970] 'Fetishism in the Horror Film', in James Donald (ed.) *Fantasy and the Cinema*, London: BFI.

De Lauretis, Teresa (1984) *Alice Doesn't: Feminism, Semiotics, Cinema*, Bloomington: Indiana University Press.

—— (1987) *Technologies of Gender: Essays on Theory, Film, and Fiction*, Bloomington: Indiana University Press.

—— (1989) 'The Essence of the Triangle or, Taking the Risk of Essentialism Seriously: Feminist Theory in Italy, the U.S., and Britain', *Differences: A Journal of Feminist Cultural Studies* 1: 3–37.

—— (1990) 'Guerrilla in the Midst: Women's Cinema in the 80s', *Screen* 31: 6–25.

—— (1991a) 'Queer Theory: Lesbian and Gay Sexualities', *Differences: A Journal of Feminist Cultural Studies* 3.2: iii–xviii.

—— (1991b) 'Film and the Visible', in Bad Object-Choices (ed.) *How Do I Look: Queer Film and Video*, Seattle: Bay Press.

—— (1994) *The Practice of Love: Lesbian Sexuality and Perverse Desire*, Bloomington: Indiana University Press.

—— (2000) [1988] 'Sexual Indifference and Lesbian Representation', in E. Ann Kaplan (ed.) *Feminism and Film*, Oxford: Oxford University Press.

—— (2003), 'When Lesbians Were Not Women', Online, Available HTTP: <http://www.unb.br/ih/his/gefem/special/delauretis.htm> (accessed 5 May 2005).

—— (2005) 'Théoriser, dit-elle', author's manuscript.

Deleuze, Gilles (1997) [1967] 'Coldness and Cruelty', in *Masochism*, trans. Jean McNeil, New York: Zone Books.

Doane, Mary Ann (1987) *The Desire to Desire: The Woman's Film of the 1940s*, Bloomington: Indiana University Press.

—— (1991) [1982] 'Film and the Masquerade: Theorizing the Female Spectator', in *Femmes Fatales: Feminism, Film Theory, Psychoanalysis*, New York: Routledge.

Dyer, Richard (ed.) (1977) *Gays and Film*, London: BFI.

Ellsworth, Elizabeth (1990) [1986] 'Illicit Pleasures: Feminist Spectators and *Personal Best*', in Patricia Erens (ed.) *Issues in Feminist Film Criticism*, Bloomington: Indiana University Press.

Firestone, Shulamith (1979) [1970], *The Dialectic of Sex: The Case for Feminist Revolution*, London: Women's Press.

Foucault, Michel (1977) [1975] *Discipline and Punish: The Birth of the Prison*, trans. Alan Sheridan, London: Allen Lane.

—— (1998) [1976] *The History of Sexuality Vol. 1: The Will to Knowledge*, trans. Robert Hurley, London: Penguin.

Freud, Sigmund (1991a) [1900] *The Interpretation of Dreams: The Penguin Freud Library*, Vol. 4, trans. James Strachey, London: Penguin.

—— (1991b) [1905] 'Three Essays on the Theory of Sexuality', in *On Sexuality: the Penguin Freud Library*, Vol. 7, trans. James Strachey, London: Penguin.

—— (1991c) [1915] 'Instincts and their Vicissitudes', in *On Metapsychology: The Penguin Freud Library*, Vol. 11, trans. James Strachey, London: Penguin.

—— (1955) [1940] 'Medusa's Head', in *The Standard Edition of the Complete Psychological Works of Sigmund Freud*, Vol. 18, trans. James Strachey, London: Hogarth Press.

Friedan, Betty (2001) [1963] *The Feminine Mystique*, New York: Norton.

Gaines, Jane (2000) [1988] 'White Privilege and Looking Relations: Race and Gender in Feminist Film Theory', in E. Ann Kaplan (ed.) *Feminism and Film*, Oxford: Oxford University Press.

Gledhill, Christine (ed.) (1987) *Home is Where the Heart is: Studies in Melodrama and the Woman's Film*, London: BFI.

Guerrilla Girls (2003) 'The Trent L'Ottscar', Online. Available HTTP: <http://www.guerrillagirls.com/posters/trent.shtml> (accessed 29 September 2005).

Hansen, Miriam (2000) [1986] 'Pleasure, Ambivalence, Identification: Valentino and Female Spectatorship', in E. Ann Kaplan (ed.) *Feminism and Film*, Oxford: Oxford University Press.

Haskell, Molly (1975) [1974] *From Reverence to Rape: The Treatment of Women in the Movies*, New York: Rinehart and Winston.

hooks, bell (1992) *Black Looks: Race and Representation*, London: Turnaround.

Irigaray, Luce (1985) [1977] *This Sex Which is Not One*, Ithaca, N.Y.: Cornell University Press.

Jayamanne, Laleen (ed.) (1995) *Kiss Me Deadly: Feminism and Cinema for the Moment*, Sydney: Power Publications.

Jeffords, Susan (1989) *The Remasculinization of America: Gender and the Vietnam War*, Bloomington: Indiana University Press.

Johnston, Claire (1973a) *Notes on Women's Cinema*, London: Society for Education in Film and Television.

—— (1973b) 'Women's Cinema as Counter-Cinema', in E. Ann Kaplan (ed.) *Feminism and Film*, Oxford: Oxford University Press.

Kaplan, E. Ann (ed.) (2000) *Feminism and Film*, Oxford: Oxford University Press.

Kim, Kyung Hyun (2004) *The Remasculinization of Korean Cinema*, Durham: Duke University Press.

Kracauer, Siegfried (1974) [1947] *From Caligari to Hitler*, Princeton, N.J.: Princeton University Press.

Kristeva, Julia (1982) [1980] *Powers of Horror: An Essay on Abjection*, New York: Columbia University Press.

Kuhn, Annette (1994) [1982] *Women's Pictures: Feminism and Cinema*, London: Verso.

Lacan, Jacques (1993) *Écrits: a selection*, trans. Alan Sheridan, London: Routledge.

—— (1994) *The Four Fundamental Concepts of Psychoanalysis*, trans. Alan Sheridan, London: Penguin.

Laplanche, Jean and Pontalis, J-B. (1968) [1964] 'Fantasy and the Origins of Sexuality', *The International Journal of Psychoanalysis* 49: 1–18.

Lauzen, Martha (2005) 'The Celluloid Ceiling: Behind-the-Scenes Employment of Women in the Top 250 Films of 2004', Online. Available HTTP: <http://www.moviesbywomen.com/marthalauzenphd/stats2004.html> (accessed 29 June 2005).

Lévi-Strauss, Claude (1969) [1949] *The Elementary Structures of Kinship*, trans. James Hurle Bell and John Richard Sturmer, London: Eyre and Spottiswoode.

Marx, Karl and Engels, Friedrich (1998) [1845–6] *The German Ideology*, Amherst, N.Y.: Prometheus Books.

Mellen, Joan (1974) *Women and their Sexuality in the New Film*, London: Davis Poynter.

Metz, Christian (1975) 'The Imaginary Signifier', *Screen* 16.2: 14–76.

Millett, Kate (1977) [1969] *Sexual Politics*, London: Virago.

Mitchell, Juliet (1966) 'Women: The Longest Revolution', *New Left Review* 40: 11–37.

—— (1977) [1971] *Woman's Estate*, Harmondsworth: Penguin.

—— (1990) [1974] *Psychoanalysis and Feminism*, London: Penguin.

Modleski, Tania (1991) *Feminism Without Women*, New York: Routledge.

Mohanna, Christine (1972), 'A One-sided story: Women in the Movies', *Women and Film* 1: 7–12.

Moi, Toril (1991) [1985] *Sexual/Textual Politics: Feminist Literary Theory*, London: Routledge.

Morgan, Robin (1970) *Sisterhood is Powerful: An Anthology of Writings from the Women's Movement*, New York: Random House.

Mulvey, Laura (1989a) 'Introduction', in *Visual and Other Pleasures*, Basingstoke: Macmillan.

—— (1989b) [1973] 'Fears, Fantasies and the Male Unconscious or "You Don't Know What is Happening, Do You, Mr Jones?"', in *Visual and Other Pleasures*, Basingstoke: Macmillan.

—— (1989c) [1975] 'Visual Pleasure and Narrative Cinema', in *Visual and Other Pleasures*, Basingstoke: Macmillan.

—— (1989d) [1981] 'Afterthoughts on "Visual Pleasure and Narrative Cinema" inspired by King Vidor's *Duel in the Sun* (1946)', in *Visual and Other Pleasures*, Basingstoke: Macmillan.

—— (1989e) [1977] 'Notes on Sirk and Melodrama', in *Visual and Other Pleasures*, Basingstoke: Macmillan.

—— (1996) *Fetishism and Curiosity*, London: BFI.

—— (1998a) 'Hollywood Cinema and Feminist Theory: A Strange but Persistent Relationship', *Iris* 26: 23–31.

—— (1998b) 'Kiarostami's Uncertainty Principle', *Sight and Sound* 8.6: 24–7.

—— (2002) 'Afterword', in Richard Tapper (ed) *The New Iranian Cinema: Politics, Representation, and Identity*, London and New York: I.B. Tauris.

—— (2005) *Death 24 × a Second: Stillness and the Moving Image*, London: Reaktion Books.

Mulvey, Laura and Jimenez, Margarita (1989) [1970] 'The Spectacle is Vulnerable: Miss World, 1970', in *Visual and Other Pleasures*, Basingstoke: Macmillan.

Naficy, Hamid (1994) 'Veiled Vision/Powerful Presences: Women in Post-revolutionary Iranian Cinema', in Mahnaz Afkhami and Erika Riedl (eds) *In the Eye of the Storm: Women in Post-revolutionary Iran*, London: I.B. Taurus.

Penley, Constance and Willis, Sharon (1988) 'Editorial: Male Trouble', *Camera Obscura* 17: 4–5.

Pick, Anat (2004) 'New Queer Cinema and Lesbian Films', in Michele Aaron (ed.) *New Queer Cinema: A Critical Reader*, Edinburgh: Edinburgh University Press.

Pisters, Patricia (2003) *The Matrix of Visual Culture: Working with Deleuze in Film Theory*, Stanford: Stanford University Press.

Propp, Vladimir (1968) [1928] *Morphology of the Folktale*, trans. Laurence Scott, Austin: University of Texas Press.

Rich, Adrienne (1983) [1980] 'Compulsory Heterosexuality and Lesbian Existence', in Elizabeth Abel and Emily K. Abel (eds) *The Signs Reader: Women, Gender and Scholarship*, Chicago: Chicago University Press.

Rivière, Joan (1986) [1929] 'Womanliness as a Masquerade', in Victor Burgin, James Donald and Cora Kaplan (eds) *Formations of Fantasy*, London: Methuen.

Rodowick, D.N. (1989) 'Reply to *Camera Obscura* on the Question of the Female Spectator', *Camera Obscura* 20–21: 269–74.

—— (2000) [1982] 'The Difficulty of Difference', in E. Ann Kaplan (ed.) *Feminism and Film*, Oxford: Oxford University Press.

Rosen, Marjorie (1973) *Popcorn Venus*, New York: Coward, McCann, and Geoghegan.

Saul, Jennifer (2003) *Feminism: Issues and Arguments*, Oxford: Oxford University Press.

Silverman, Kaja (1980) 'Masochism and Subjectivity', *Framework* 12: 2–9.

—— (1983) *The Subject of Semiotics*, New York: Oxford University Press.

—— (1988) *The Acoustic Mirror: The Female Voice in Psychoanalysis and Cinema*, Bloomington: Indiana University Press.

—— (1990) [1984] 'Dis-embodying the Female Voice', in Patricia Erens (ed.) *Issues in Feminist Film Criticism*, Bloomington: Indiana University Press.

—— (1992) *Male Subjectivity at the Margins*, New York: Routledge.

—— (1996) *Threshold of the Visible World*, London: Routledge.

Stacey, Jackie (2000) [1987] 'Desperately Seeking Difference', in E. Ann Kaplan (ed.) *Feminism and Film*, Oxford: Oxford University Press.

Tarratt, Margaret (1995) [1971] 'Monsters from the Id', in Barry Keith Grant (ed.) *Film Genre II*, Austin: University of Texas Press.

Wittig, Monique (1992) *The Straight Mind and Other Essays*, Boston: Beacon Press.

Wollen, Peter (1972) *Signs and Meanings in the Cinema*, Bloomington: Indiana University Press.

Wollstonecraft, Mary (1992) [1792] *Vindication of the Rights of Woman*, London: Penguin.

Wood, Robin (1978) 'The Return of the Repressed', *Film Comment* 14.4: 25–32.

—— (1986) *Hollywood From Vietnam to Reagan*, New York: Columbia University Press.

INDEX